A Unique Publishing Venture

This is a new, revised edition of a handbook which was first published in 1958. *A Parent's Guide to Children's Reading* was a unique publishing venture which was initiated by the National Book Committee in an effort to encourage more children to read more widely. The National Book Committee, Inc., is an independent, nonprofit organization which seeks to foster the wiser and wider use of books. Recognizing the need for a new, comprehensive handbook for parents on their children's reading, the Committee began in 1956 to make arrangements for the preparation and publication of such a book. A highly qualified author was chosen and help was sought from leading professional and civic groups.

National organizations representing children, parents, librarians, teachers, and others concerned with children's reading accepted the invitation to cooperate. Each group named a consultant to advise the author in the area in which he was particularly qualified. Each group also helped to introduce the book to thousands of parents. *A Parent's Guide to Children's Reading* was published on a nonprofit basis in two editions, a hardcover edition published by Doubleday & Company, Inc., and a paperback edition published by Pocket Books, Inc. More than half a million copies of the first edition were sold, and profits were turned over to the National Book Committee for continuing work in the field of reading development.

Five years later, the success of the 1958 edition brought many requests for a new, revised edition containing up-to-date information. The National Book Committee again turned to the cooperating organizations, and their consultants have again worked with the author.

These consultants and the organizations they represent are:

Betsy H. Angert, Adult Education Association

Rachael W. DeAngelo, American Association of School Librarians, a division of the American Library Association and a department of the National Education Association

Nora E. Beust, American Association of University Women

Robert S. Fleming, Association for Childhood Education International

Harry A. Harchar, Boy Scouts of America

Iris Vinton, Boys' Clubs of America

Margaret Mary Kelly, Camp Fire Girls, Inc.

Clara J. Kircher, Catholic Library Association.

Josette Frank, Child Study Association of America

Laura Cathon, Children's Services Division of the American Library Association.

Geraldine Fenn, 4-H Clubs

Mrs. Harvey E. Johnson, General Federation of Women's Clubs

Alice White, Girl Scouts of the U.S.A.

Margaret J. Early, International Reading Association

Frances A. Sullivan, National Congress of Parents and Teachers

Helen Raebeck, National Council of Jewish Women

Elizabeth Guilfoile, National Council of Teachers of English

Thomas M. Campbell, U. S. Junior Chamber of Commerce

The author and the National Book Committee are deeply grateful to these consultants for their thoughtful contributions. At the same time, the author assumes full responsibility for the organization and content of the book.

A PARENT'S GUIDE TO CHILDREN'S READING is being published on a nonprofit basis in two editions— this paperback edition and a clothbound edition published by Doubleday & Company, Inc., at $3.95. Any profits from the sales of either of these editions will be turned over to the National Book Committee.

~~~~~~

If your regular bookseller does not have copies of the edition you want, you may order it this way:

FOR THE CLOTHBOUND EDITION: Send $3.95 to Doubleday & Company, Inc., Garden City, N.Y.

FOR THE PAPERBOUND EDITION: Send $.50, plus 10 cents per copy for handling and postage, to Pocket Books, Inc., Mail Service Department, 1 West 39th St., New York 18, N.Y.

Also by Nancy Larrick

A Parent's Guide to Children's Education
A Teacher's Guide to Children's Books

Pa
arent's
guide to
children's
reading

NANCY LARRICK

 A GIANT CARDINAL EDITION published by
POCKET BOOKS, INC. • NEW YORK

A PARENT'S GUIDE TO CHILDREN'S READING

Doubleday edition published April, 1964

A *Giant Cardinal* edition
1st printing........February, 1964

This *Giant Cardinal*** edition includes every word contained in the
hardbound edition published simultaneously by Doubleday & Company, Inc.
It is printed from brand-new plates made from
completely reset, clear, easy-to-read type.
Giant Cardinal editions are published by Pocket Books, Inc., and
are printed and distributed in the U.S.A. by Affiliated Publishers,
a division of Pocket Books, Inc., 630 Fifth Avenue, New York 20, N.Y.
*Trademark registered in the United States and other countries.
**Trademark of Pocket Books, 630 Fifth
Avenue, New York 20, N.Y., in the United States   L
and other countries.

ACKNOWLEDGMENTS

Grateful acknowledgment is made to the following for permission
to use copyrighted material:

THE BODLEY HEAD LTD.: For an illustration by Richard Kennedy
from *The Horse Without a Head* (English title: *A Hundred Million
Francs*) by Paul Berna.

COWARD-MCCANN, INC.: For an illustration by Kurt Wiese from
The Five Chinese Brothers by Claire Huchet Bishop and Kurt
Wiese, copyright 1938 by Coward-McCann, Inc.; for an illustration by Wanda Gág from *Millions of Cats* by Wanda Gág, copyright 1928 by Coward-McCann, Inc.

THOMAS Y. CROWELL COMPANY: For an illustration by Walter H. Lorraine in *A Little Laughter*, copyright © 1957 by Katherine Love, the compiler.

DOUBLEDAY & COMPANY, INC.: For an illustration by Leonard Weisgard from *Favorite Poems Old and New* selected by Helen Ferris, copyright © 1957 by Helen Ferris Tibbets.

E. P. DUTTON & CO., INC.: For an illustration by E. H. Shepard from *When We Were Very Young* by A. A. Milne. Copyright 1924 by E. P. Dutton & Co., Inc. Renewal 1952 by A. A. Milne.

FARRAR, STRAUS AND COMPANY, INC.: For an illustration by Garth Williams from *The Cricket in Times Square* by George Selden. Copyright © 1960 by George Selden Thompson and Garth Williams.

HARCOURT, BRACE & WORLD, INC.: For an illustration by Enrico Arno from *The King's Drum and Other African Stories* by Harold Courlander, copyright © 1962 by Harold Courlander; for an illustration from *Nu Dang and His Kite* by Jacqueline Ayer, copyright © 1959 by Jacqueline Ayer; for an illustration by N. M. Bodecker from *Half Magic* by Edward Eager, copyright 1954 by Harcourt, Brace & World, Inc.; for an illustration by Beth and Joe Krush from *Gone-Away Lake* by Elizabeth Enright, copyright © 1957 by Elizabeth Enright; for an illustration by Nicolas Mordvinoff from *The Two Reds* by Will and Nicolas, copyright 1950 by Will Lipkind and Nicolas Mordvinoff; for an illustration by Nicolas from *Alphonse That Bearded One* by Natalie Savage Carlson, copyright 1954 by Harcourt, Brace & World, Inc.

HARPER & ROW, PUBLISHERS, INCORPORATED: For an illustration by Syd Hoff from *Danny and the Dinosaur* by Syd Hoff, copyright © 1958 by Syd Hoff; for an illustration by Winifred Lubell from *See Through the Forest* by Millicent Selsam, copyright © 1956 by Harper & Row, Publishers, Incorporated; for an illustration by Leonard Shortall from *A Dog on Barkham Street* by M. S. Stoltz, copyright © 1960 by M. S. Stoltz; for an illustration by Tomi Ungerer from *Crictor* by Tomi Ungerer, copyright © 1958 by Jean Thomas Ungerer; for an illustration by Garth Williams from *Charlotte's Web* by E. B. White, copyright 1952 by E. B. White.

LITTLE, BROWN AND COMPANY, INC.: For an illustration by Leonard Everett Fisher from *Mike Fink* by James Cloyd Bowman, copyright © 1957 by James Cloyd Bowman; for an illustration by Robert Lawson from *Mr. Popper's Penguins* by Richard and Florence Atwater, copyright 1938 by Richard and Florence Atwater; for an illustration by Artur Marokvia from *The Happy Days* by Kim Yong Ik, copyright © 1960 by Kim Yong Ik; for an illustration from *Favorite Fairy Tales Told in Germany* retold by Virginia Haviland, illustrations copyright © 1959 by Susanne Suba.

McGRAW-HILL-WHITTLESEY HOUSE: For an illustration by Roger Duvoisin from *The Happy Lion* by Louise Fatio, copyright 1954 by Louise Fatio Duvoisin and Roger Duvoisin; for an illustration by Paul Galdone from *Miss Pickerell Goes to Mars* by Ellen MacGregor, copyright 1951 by Ellen MacGregor; for an illustration by Ezra Jack Keats from *Danny Dunn and the Anti-Gravity Paint* by Jay Williams and Raymond Abrashkin, copyright © 1956 by Jay Williams and Raymond Abrashkin.

RANDOM HOUSE, INC.: For an illustration by Rudolf Freund from *All About Snakes* by Bessie M. Hecht, © copyright 1956 by Bessie M. Hecht; for an illustration by Dr. Seuss from *The Cat in the Hat* by Dr. Seuss, © copyright 1957 by Dr. Seuss; for an illustration by John Wright from *I had a little . . .* by Norma Levarie, © copyright 1961 by Norma Levarie.

WILLIAM R. SCOTT, INC.: For an illustration by Dagmar Wilson from *Casey the Utterly Impossible Horse* by Anita Feagles, copyright © 1960 by Anita Macrae Feagles.

CHARLES SCRIBNER'S SONS: For an illustration by Helen Sewell from *The Bears on Hemlock Mountain* by Alice Dalgliesh, copyright © 1957 by Alice Dalgliesh.

THE VIKING PRESS, INC.: For an illustration by Louis S. Glanzman from *Pippi Longstocking* by Astrid Lindgren, copyright 1950 by The Viking Press, Inc.; for an illustration by Kazue Mizumura from *The Cheerful Heart* by Elizabeth Janet Gray, copyright © 1959 by Elizabeth Janet Gray.

HENRY Z. WALCK, INC.: For an illustration by William Stobbs from *The Gorgon's Head: The Story of Perseus* by Ian Serraillier, copyright © 1961 by Ian Serraillier.

FRANKLIN WATTS, INC.: For an illustration by Ursula Koering from *This Boy Cody* by Leon Wilson, copyright 1950 by Leon Wilson.

THE WORLD PUBLISHING COMPANY: For an illustration by Rainey Bennett from *The Secret Hiding Place* by Rainey Bennett, copyright © 1960 by Rainey Bennett.

To These
My Special Thanks

MANY of my friends have been unofficial consultants in the writing of this handbook for parents. Their encouragement and their practical suggestions have helped tremendously. To these loyal ones, especially, I express my deep appreciation:

Daniel Melcher, publisher of *Library Journal*, who first pointed out the need for this kind of book, who kept the project warm when others were uncertain, and who suggested using illustrations from children's books.

Dr. Alvina Burrows, Professor of Education at New York University, who was chairman of my doctoral committee and supervised the research project which laid the foundation for this handbook.

Margaret W. Dudley and Marchette Chute, representing the National Book Committee, who provided moral support when it was most needed and who have worked steadily to give the project nationwide publicity.

My husband, Alexander L. Crosby, who gave valuable editorial assistance in writing and revising the manuscript.

Margaret Walp, who typed and retyped the manuscript with remarkable patience and efficiency.

And my father and mother, who used to read to me every evening and thus set a pattern for *A Parent's Guide to Children's Reading*.

NANCY LARRICK

Quakertown, Pennsylvania
September 1963

Contents

III: Getting the Books He Needs

IV: Books and Magazines for Children

V: Further Reading for Parents

A Parent's guide to children's reading

Dear
Parents . . .

WHEN PARENTS talk about their children's reading, they almost invariably ask, "What can we do to help?"

The answer depends upon you and your child, of course. But you can be sure that you have tremendous potential influence.

Every time you read aloud to the child or let him browse through a picture book, he sees that you are interested in reading. When you visit the library or invite him to tell about library books he has borrowed, he knows that reading is important to you. From your example, he will conclude that reading is a pleasure. In this receptive state of mind, he will learn more easily and quickly at school.

Equally important is the fact that through reading he grows and develops as a person. Even at the pat-a-cake age, a child's personality begins to expand when he hears the old nursery rhymes.

If you provide him with continuing delight in reading, you are helping him develop as a happy, self-sufficient person. Through books, he may visit different lands and different ages; he may explore science and art; he may face up to critical issues. If you encourage him to ask questions and get to the root of what he reads, his reading will help him become a thinking citizen.

People in storybooks become part of his real world. There is Michael, the policeman in **Make Way for Ducklings,** whose compassion for the ducklings made him stop traffic on a busy street. And the web-writing spider in

3

Charlotte's Web, who wins glory for a pig. There is Henry Huggins, whose guppies multiplied so fast they almost crowded him out of his room. And the Moffat family which goes merrily on despite a limited budget.

These are friends to enjoy. But they are friends who start children thinking too. As a child reads such stories—and there are hundreds more—he is beginning to establish his pattern of values. His respect for other people is taking shape. His sensitivity is growing. His own satisfaction is making him a more secure person. And by his questions and his comparisons he is becoming a more creative thinker.

Your influence in this unfolding process is tremendous, perhaps even greater than the teacher's. You are with the child much more, and your example will influence him all his life.

The guidance you give in reading will be more effective if it is in harmony with the guidance the teacher is giving. It is important for you to get acquainted with the teacher. Each of you has ideas and information that will help the other. The teacher can explain how reading is taught at school. From her experience with books and children, she can suggest stories your child will like. And from your intimate experience you can help her know your young one better.

A PARENT'S GUIDE TO CHILDREN'S READING describes specific activities which may help children to read with greater skill and with continuing pleasure. All of the suggestions are made in the light of what is known about the way children grow and the way they learn. In every case I have tried to spell out the reason why a certain procedure is recommended.

You will see that this handbook is organized into five sections.

Part I, "How You Can Help, Day In and Day Out," gives suggestions for reading aloud, for introducing books and stories, for stirring the child's curiosity, and for talking things over with him. Since the suggestions are given in chapters relating to different age levels, you may wish to turn at once to the chapter which tells about helping your child now. But if you wonder how he got where he is, start with Chapter 1, "Begin When He Is a Baby."

Part II, "How Reading Is Taught Today," is for those who want to know more about how children learn and how they are taught to read. This section gives more detailed reasons behind the recommendations in Part I.

Part III, "Getting the Books He Needs," gives suggestions on how to use the library, how to develop a home library, and how to buy books.

Part IV, "Books and Magazines for Children," is an annotated list of children's books, plus a directory of publishers. There is also a list of magazines—both juvenile and adult—which children enjoy.

Part V lists books and pamphlets that give further information about children's reading.

Thus the last two parts of the handbook are working tools that you can turn to again and again for specific help.

Part I.

How You Can Help, Day In and Day Out

in certain words you could never be

to play

1.

Begin When He Is a Baby

Even a baby likes the sound of a friendly voice. He doesn't understand the words, of course. He may be too young to talk. But he can coo and gurgle and kick his feet. It's his way of talking, and he enjoys it.

By the time he is eight or nine months old, a baby will show delight in simple nursery rhymes and games. He will squeal with pleasure when he hears one of his old favorites: "This little pig went to market" or "Pat-a-cake, pat-a-cake."

Each day he will join in a bit more until finally he is lisping the words and beating time. Later he will enjoy such simple singing games as "I Turn Myself Around."

Getting Ready to Read

When you enjoy these games with your baby, you may not be thinking of books and reading. Nevertheless, you are making a real start in getting your child ready for reading. He is experimenting with his voice in response to your conversation. He is hearing words that rhyme and lines that repeat themselves. As he claps, he is getting a feeling for the rhythm and music of language. Above all, he is finding that this delights him to his very toes.

If you had tried to prepare a child for reading by drilling him on a list of words, you could never have created such an air of enchantment. When you play "pat-a-cake," you are doing something much subtler and much more important.

Many of the experiences of a young child can influence his approach to reading. Most important, they may affect his later enjoyment of reading.

Children who become good readers are often those who think and talk well. From his youngest days, then, help your child to think and talk. And the more fun he has while learning, the better. (But remember that children differ. Some who are poor talkers become good readers later on.)

Even in his carriage days, a baby should have the opportunity for conversation. At first you may feel you are doing all the talking. But by his smiles and sounds, he soon gets in on the act.

If he hears language at this early stage he is likely to develop his own skills more rapidly. So your first play with the baby should include lots of talk—nursery rhymes and jingles as well as spontaneous conversation. If you have forgotten the old rhymes, get a Mother Goose book and brush up on your favorites. (See pages 14 to 15 for a list of Mother Goose books.)

Also refresh your memory on the words and music of some of the old nursery songs. One nice little collection entitled **Favorite Nursery Songs,** compiled by Phyllis Brown Ohanian, contains words with music and delightful pictures. Another lovely book that includes nursery songs and lullabies in the **New Golden Song Book,** compiled by Norman Lloyd.*

√ *Children love to play with sounds.* Sometimes they hear words that imitate sounds, such as *bow-wow* and *bumpety-bump.* They like to repeat these words. Often

*Each children's book mentioned in the text is described in more detail (with price and publisher) in Part IV, "Books and Magazines for Children."

they will say them over and over as though enjoying the music.

Or they will try to make new sounds from old. Sometimes a child will begin a sort of chain of words, one growing out of the other. *Clickety-clack* may suggest *clackety-clack* and then a long string of *clack, clack, clack, clack, clack*. The child seems to be playing with the sounds. And all the time he is learning to distinguish between sounds that are very much alike or easily confused. He is developing a sharp ear for differences. All of this will help him with his talking and, later, with his reading.

√ *Children like repetition of sound.* Perhaps that is one reason why they like nursery rhymes so much, for these old rhymes repeat themselves constantly. Consider this old timer:

> *Polly, put the kettle on*
> *Polly, put the kettle on*
> *Polly, put the kettle on*
> *And we'll all have tea.*
>
> *Sukey, take it off again*
> *Sukey, take it off again*
> *Sukey, take it off again*
> *They've all gone away.*

There's not much plot to that story. Yet children love it for its repetition. As soon as your child begins to talk a bit, he will probably want to say some of these lines with you. The repetition will make him sure he is right, and he will like that too.

For more fun of this sort, try such a poem as "Over in the Meadow." Words and music are in the beautiful picture book of the same title, illustrated by Feodor Rojankovsky.

Over in the meadow in the sand in the sun,
Lived an old mother turtle and her little turtle one.
Dig, said the mother. We dig, said the one.
So they dug all day in the sand in the sun.

Every stanza tells about a different mother animal, but each begins "Over in the meadow." The third line always gives the mother's command and the baby's reply.

After hearing this nursery song several times, the child may be able to sing part of it with you. For example, you might sing the words of the old mother fish: "*Swim,* said the mother." Then he can chime in with "*We swim,* said the two."

Even when he is very young, a child may begin to understand the drama and delight that come from stories and books.

Reading Aloud to the Very Young

At eight or nine months, a baby will usually enjoy nursery songs and lullabies. By twelve or fourteen months, he may look at pictures while nursery rhymes are read or sung. By one and a half or two years, he may turn the pages himself. Soon he knows each story so well he can correct your slightest slip.

If your child comes to these pleasures much later, there is no cause for worry. Each child has his own time schedule.

When you have read aloud to a child a great deal, you will understand what delight it gives to the child. And if you are completely honest, you will admit you have enjoyed it just about as much.

Few activities create a warmer relationship between child and grownup than reading aloud. It is deeply flattering to be read to and have the undivided attention of an adult.

Many parents plan a regular time for reading aloud each day. Just before nap time and just before bedtime are traditional choices. Whatever the hour, be sure to make it the same each day so the child will look forward to it as he does to lunch or supper.

You may want to start the story hour by letting the child choose the first story. If he asks you to read this story again, by all means do it. Let him revel in the familiar. Then introduce a new story. Give him a chance to ask about it and play with the words and ideas. It may take several readings before he responds warmly. When that happens, the book will probably be a long-time favorite.

Let the child sit where he can see the pictures and help to hold the book. If you pause at intervals, he will enjoy looking for particular things in the pictures. But at first he may need some encouragement.

Three-year-old Jimmie was at that stage when I first read him **Make Way for Ducklings**. I could tell he was pleased, but he sat silent and motionless. So on the second go-round, I paused from time to time to ask a question. "Where are the little ducklings, Jimmie? Let's point to each one." He took the cue and began to point. Then I asked if he saw a baby carriage in the park. Jimmie looked for a long time and then squealed, "There it is!" Soon he was pointing out details on his own or asking if I saw some small object in the background. This was probably the first time he had been an active participant in reading, and he loved it. The benefit was partly in his feeling that he too could read.

You will not always be so lucky in bringing child and book together. Sometimes the young listener gets restless and bored. Maybe the book is not right or the time is not right. If he wants to get on with a particular book instead of lingering over the pictures, by all means let him. He may turn several pages at once in order to finish a story that does not interest him. Or he may clearly show he would rather play outdoors. Respect his mood and his choice; let reading wait until he wants it.

Perhaps the time will come when you are away and the baby sitter is in charge. Prepare her by leaving a few favorite books and giving her some hints about reading aloud.

Books for Children under Four

No book can be recommended absolutely for any age. Sometimes a book that is just right for one three-year-old seems too advanced or too babyish for another. Often a book that is adored at three may remain the child's favorite for several years.

The following books are suggested because they have been popular with many children. Notice the art work in these books. The drawings are simple and the colors are clear. The pages avoid the cluttered, busy look that spoils some books.

NURSERY RHYMES are available in books of all sizes and all prices. Buy at least one book of nursery rhymes that is a thing of beauty. Children sense the special quality of such a book. They quickly learn to handle it carefully.

The Real Mother Goose, illustrated by Blanche Fisher Wright, is one of the most popular editions. It has colorful pictures on every page—pictures so clear and simple that they appeal to the young child.

The Tall Book of Mother Goose gets its name from its shape—about 12 inches tall and 5 inches wide. It contains about 100 well-loved rhymes, illustrated by Feodor Rojankovsky with very gay, humorous pictures in bold colors. The children are pictured as husky modern youngsters in everyday play clothes, with pets that look wonderfully real.

Book of Nursery and Mother Goose Rhymes, compiled and illustrated by Marguerite de Angeli, is a big, lavishly beautiful volume with many illustrations in soft colors and a wealth of nursery rhymes.

Mother Goose, illustrated by Tasha Tudor, is best known for its dainty illustrations in soft colors. The selection of verses is excellent.

Ring o' Roses, illustrated by L. Leslie Brooke, is a perennial favorite. It has only about 20 rhymes, but the pictures are unforgettable.

Mother Goose, illustrated by Corinne Malvern, costs only a dollar and is a good buy at that price. It has full-color illustrations and over 90 favorite rhymes.

BEDTIME STORIES are always welcome and often have a quieting effect after a busy day. Several very popular ones tell of the coming of darkness and bedtime.

A Child's Good Night Book, by Margaret Wise Brown, shows one group of animals after another at bedtime—birds, wild monkeys, squirrels, and kangaroos among many others. At the end children, too, "say their prayers, get under the covers and go to sleep" with the final prayer:

> *Dear Father*
> *hear and bless*
> *thy beasts and*
> *singing birds.*
> *And guard with*
> *tenderness*
> *small things*
> *that have*
> *no words.*

Goodnight Moon, also by Margaret Wise Brown, is a lovely bedtime story for the very young. I have given it to children of only twelve or fourteen months. Each time the mother admitted she had thought her baby was too young for a book but before long he loved this one. Little children like the simple pictures of familiar things and the gentle repetition:

> *Goodnight bears*
> *Goodnight chairs*
> *Goodnight mittens*
> *Goodnight kittens.*

When I gave the book to Sally, she was only eighteen months old. Pretty soon she was adding goodnights of her own: "Goodnight, dolly," she would say, "and goodnight, Mommy." Each evening she added more and more goodnights as though trying to prolong the story and her own pleasure. **Goodnight Moon** was Sally's favorite book for a long time—the one she always took to bed with her.

ANIMAL STORIES are usually popular with very young children. Those with realistic pictures seem to have the greatest appeal and those with photographs are coming into great popularity.

Baby Farm Animals, by Garth Williams, makes a wonderful first book. The full-color pictures show young animals frisking and cavorting—dogs, kittens, ducks, chicks, and all the rest. The text is brief and gay.

Make Way for Ducklings, by Robert McCloskey, has become a favorite of all ages. It is the story of a family of mallard ducks in Boston, how they find a home and are befriended by a policeman. The bold illustrations tell much of the story.

The Duck consists of gorgeous photographs by Ylla and simple text by Margaret Wise Brown. The story tells

And now he saw a fuzzy grey kitten down in the corner and he took her too.

From Millions of Cats, *written and illustrated by Wanda Gág (Coward-McCann, Inc.)*

of a duck that visits the zoo, so the photographs show many animals.

Millions of Cats, by Wanda Gág, is an established favorite of children and adults. A very old man and a very old woman wanted a cat—just one cat—but soon they had "millions and billions and trillions of cats."

The Tale of Peter Rabbit, by Beatrix Potter, has become so beloved since it was published in 1903 that parents and grandparents know it almost by heart.

Johnny Crow's Garden, by L. Leslie Brooke, is a delightful old story of the garden planted and tended by Johnny Crow and visited by all kinds of animals. Each page has only a line or two of rhyming text.

Harry the Dirty Dog, by Gene Zion, is the story of a white dog with black spots who gets himself so dirty that his owners don't know him. His early objection to a bath disappears, and he makes an amusing struggle to be clean again.

The Story About Ping, by Marjorie Flack, concerns a fluffy little yellow duck that lives on a Chinese river boat. Each day Ping and his family go ashore. When Ping strays, his adventures begin.

NURSERY TALES are popular with almost every three-year-old.

Established favorites include **The Little Red Hen, Chicken Licken, The Three Little Pigs,** and **The Three Bears.** Each is a real story with characters and a plot. Repetition adds to the suspense. Thus, in **The Three Little Pigs** the greedy wolf makes the same request each time:

"Little pig, little pig, let me in, let me in!"

And each time he makes the same threat:

"I'll huff and I'll puff and I'll blow your house in!"

When a small child builds a tower of blocks, he likes to knock it down with a crash. Noisy climaxes are music to his soul. I have often thought that some of the old nursery tales appeal to children by virtue of their smash-ups. In **The Little Red Hen,** for example, a stone is rolled into the kettle with such a splash that boiling water covers the murderous fox. The wolf in **The Three Little Pigs** does himself in by jumping down the chimney into another kettle. The foolish milkmaid tosses her head, and a jar of milk crashes around her. And so it goes from one smash-up to another.

Note, too, that the little fellow usually gets the better of the big one. A plain little hen outwits a fox, a humble pig exterminates a wolf, a modest tortoise defeats a hare. Nursery fiction presents the triumph of the weaker animal. And children like that too.

Twenty-four of the most popular stories are included in **The Tall Book of Nursery Tales,** illustrated by Feodor Rojankovsky.

THE CHILD'S WORLD is shown in a number of books that young children enjoy.

Play With Me, by Marie Hall Ets, is the picture-book story of a little girl who wants someone to play with. She tries the grasshopper, the frog, the turtle, the chipmunk, and many others. As she tries to catch one, he hops away. But when she sits down quietly, each comes back to get acquainted.

Umbrella, by Taro Yashima, combines brilliant color and singing text to tell of a small Japanese girl in New York who longs for rain so she can use her new umbrella and red rubber boots.

All Falling Down, by Gene Zion, is appreciated by young children because of the reassuring surprise ending. Pictures and text tell of things that are falling down— leaves, snow, the block house. But at the end—"Daddy lifts him up and tosses him in the air. *He doesn't fall down. Daddy catches him.*"

2.

From Four to Six

The four-year-old and the five-year-old show greater interest and skill in everything related to reading than do their younger brothers and sisters. They speak more distinctly. They do a lot more talking. They ask more questions. They are beginning to be curious about printed words. The whole world is larger at four and five, and the child is trying to take it all in.

The new horizons add to his everyday fun, and they can help equip him for reading.

Tall Talk Is Good

At four, a child may be a steady talker. He talks to everybody, including the cat. Alone, he talks happily to himself. Often he repeats his questions until grownups are exhausted. Actually the constant "Why?" may be his way of keeping a friendly conversation going.

When you understand how important talking is to a child's intellectual growth, you see your role as a parent. You listen to his prattle. You encourage him to talk about what he has been doing. You meet him on his level, asking simple questions about the things he sees and does.

The child who has been brought up to be seen and not heard is often handicapped in reading. Twins are sometimes slow talkers and slow readers because they are so used to each other's company that they learn to communicate with few words. In contrast, the child who talks easily is generally better prepared for reading.

It is natural for children of this age to have fun with words. They will repeat a new word over and over as though savoring a delicate morsel. Often they indulge in spontaneous word games that sharpen their ear for oral language.

I recall such a game between four-year-old Ahnie and ten-year-old Red, who had been playing together. As Red started upstairs, these exchanges were made:

RED: See you later, alligator.

AHNIE: See you later . . . snake.

RED: You were supposed to say, "See you soon, baboon!"

AHNIE: See you soon on the moon.

RED: See you later, alligator.

AHNIE: See you later in the 'frigerator.

RED: See you later on the escalator.

AHNIE: What's an escalator?

The four-year-old caught onto the pattern of rhyme and almost vanquished her senior partner. But her interest in rhyme was sidetracked by curiosity about the new word. A child with such a sharp ear for sounds and such curiosity about meaning is likely to become an excellent reader.

Although the dialogue of Ahnie and Red was spontaneous, both children had played many word games with their parents. These games were never planned as word drills or lessons. They were simply used to pass the time on long automobile rides or rainy afternoons.

There are many word games which children enjoy.

√ *Words beginning with the same sound* can be a start-

"I'd like to have the moose," said Julian.

From Gone-Away Lake, *by Elizabeth Enright, illustrated by Beth and Joe Krush (Harcourt, Brace & World)*

er. How many words can we name that begin with the same *D* sound as Dickie? Or the *B* of Betsy or the *T* of Tom?

√ *Rhyming words* can be listed, too, with each person supplying a new word, as in *bake-cake-lake-make-rake.*

√ *Words that imitate sounds* such as *bang, pop,* and *whir* are always fun to compile—and to invent. Make notes of the best inventions.

√ *Storytelling* by children and with them will increase their ability to talk as well as strengthen their story sense. Try reading a simple story like **The Three Bears** and then suggest that the child help you retell the story. After a few tries he may want to tell the whole story himself.

√ *Playing a story* gives a child the opportunity to act

out a favorite story. A woolly scarf, a pocketbook or dress-up hat may be enough to make him feel the part he plays.

√ *Reporting on the day's events* is another way for the child to get good experience with language. Perhaps he would like to tell about the wonderful spider web he has seen.

√ *Asking questions and finding answers* should always be encouraged. At the beach, for example, gather shells and show how some are similar and some different. In the woods or in a park do the same with leaves. Speculate about them, and the child may soon be asking questions.

All of these activities bring immediate satisfaction. They may also improve the child's talking and thinking, which are steps to good reading later on.

Baby Talk

Every now and then you meet a four- or five-year-old who says *fwoo* for *through* or *booful* for *beautiful*. Usually the child could speak distinctly if given encouragement.

Children are marvelously imitative. When parents speak clearly, the child is apt to do the same. On the other hand many youngsters hang onto baby talk because the parents cling to it too. The remedy is obvious.

Most children outgrow baby talk as a matter of course. When errors persist, parents can help—provided they avoid nagging or drilling that makes the child feel at fault.

Suppose a five-year-old keeps saying *fum* for *thumb*. As a kind of game, show him where you place your tongue to make the *th* sound and how you use lips and teeth for *F*. Then he can make a try and feel the difference. If this demonstration is made before a mirror, the child can see how well he is imitating your lip movements.

Be sure he receives praise for his effort and develops a feeling of achievement.

The five-year-old who pronounces *when* and *went* alike may be confused later when he learns to read and finds those words in print. If you help your child to outgrow baby talk, you may help him to become a better reader as well.

"What Does It Say?"

In the two years before entering first grade some children become very much aware of written language. They see printed words everywhere: on cereal boxes, newspapers, letters, billboards, neon signs, the television screen. Often they associate words from two or more of these sources. Television gives the pronunciation of product names.

A few children begin to read advertising slogans and other words quite spontaneously. They can tell Shredded Wheat from Wheaties, for example, by reading the words and pictures. One precocious three-year-old of my acquaintance identified his presents under the Christmas tree by recognizing his name on the tags.

Curiosity about the meaning of words is the natural sequel to awareness. You can do extremely valuable work by welcoming this curiosity with clear-cut answers. At first the child may simply ask what a certain word is, to which the answer is "Chocolate." Later he will want to know how you know it says *chocolate*. At this point he can probably use some clues to word recognition.

At five, Fred told me he always knew the letter S when he saw it. He pointed to a big S on an aluminum salt shaker. Then he turned to a magazine and went from one advertisement to another picking out S's.

"It all began when we broke the glass salt shaker,"

Fred's mother explained later. "We began using the aluminum ones marked S and P, and you have to know the difference. So Fred learned those two letters first of all."

To help him learn, Fred's mother had started a game of "Find the letter S."

The typical five-year-old might not keep his mind on the letter S as long as Fred did. Don't be dismayed if your child gets a far-away look while you are answering a question or if he walks right out. He'll be back later.

Suppose he asks how to print his initials. Show him with big letters in crayon. Let him practice as long as he's interested, but don't force him to keep going so he can have something to show his father.

If the youngster is seriously interested in printing his whole name, there's no reason why he shouldn't. Be sure to use what is called "manuscript" writing (see pages 48 to 49), the style used in most first and second grades.

When a child asks how to print or write, he wants to learn. But if you force him to make letters he does not understand or care about, you may inhibit his interest in reading and writing later on.

Don't worry if your child shows no curiosity about reading and writing at this stage. Probably only a few children will.

Just remember that children grow and develop at different rates. Those who seem slow at first will soon catch up. Give your child time and a warm feeling that what he's doing is fine with you. There is only one hard and fast rule: Don't push, lest you slow down the child's interest and inclination to learn.

Broadening Children's Interests

Four- and five-year-olds are ready to explore anything and everything. They stick their noses into closets and boxes. They pull up tiny radish plants. No matter how exasperating, this natural curiosity should be fostered. It is the child's way of seeking information and broader horizons.

What does this have to do with reading? Everything. Through his natural desire to find out, the child gets the background that will give meaning to his reading in later years. Unknowingly he is preparing for reading when he asks question after question. When he starts school, he will be full of ideas to talk about and write about. When he reads, he will have much to bring to the printed page. And he will have developed the habit of looking for new ideas and new experiences.

Your reaction to the curiosity of your four- or five-year-old may influence him for the rest of his life. If you brush aside his questions, he may conclude that questions are bad and exploration should be discontinued. Yet these are the very things you wish to foster.

Here are some of the areas in which you can provide new experiences:

√ *Acquiring a pet.* That decision will bring satisfaction, entertainment and a considerable amount of education. The animal gives much to talk about and read about. (See pages 30 to 31 for animal stories popular at this age.)

√ *Planting seeds.* Even a few nasturtium seeds in a pot or a row of lettuce or radishes in the yard will provide suspense and excitement. (Lettuce is a prudent choice because it should be pulled up early.) With a garden of their own, children may become more interested in all plant life and have more questions to ask.

√ *Local visits.* The visit can be to the supermarket or the post office or the dairy. With just a little extra time, you can take the child behind the scenes or let him linger where he wishes. The railroad terminal and the airport are always exciting, and there's fascination in a hatchery.

Give the child plenty of time to take in the sights and sounds and smells and ask all the questions he can think of.

✓ *Short trips.* No passports are required. In fact it may be better to visit only the monkey house at the zoo than to take in too much. City dwellers may find a wonderful barnyard only a short drive from town—or a woods carpeted with spring beauties and dogtooth violets. Suburban children will thrill over a trip on a city subway or through dense city traffic.

✓ *Television.* Only a few television programs are designed for children under six. Several of these come on during the morning rush hour when small children especially welcome entertainment. Take time to identify such programs on your local TV schedule and introduce them to your pre-schoolers.

Often children broaden their interests and increase their vocabularies through television, especially if they can talk about what they have seen. With encouragement they will seek answers to new questions, thus laying a good foundation for reading. (See Chapter 8, "Television and Children's Reading.")

✓ *Adult magazines.* Exploring picture magazines is good entertainment any day. The four-year-old may spread a large magazine on the floor and crawl from side to side to study pictures.

✓ *Scrapbooks.* It may be a snapshot album or a paste-in scrapbook, but if it relates to the child it will be treasured. At five, Fred could explain every snapshot in his album, including the one labeled "My Second Christmas," in which he was gnawing a turkey leg. Betsy had a scrapbook of kitten pictures from magazines and newspapers, each labeled by her mother, as the child directed.

✓ *Talking it over.* Whatever the new interest or experience, it is often more valuable if talked about. When you are on the spot, help the child see things he might overlook. Answer his questions simply and briefly. Remember that some children like to mull over their experiences and do their talking later.

Reading Aloud to Fours and Fives

Not long ago a "Reading-Aloud Shelf" was set up in a Tennessee factory. It had picture books which the workers were invited to borrow for reading aloud to their children. In two days the shelf was bare. On the third day books began trickling back and going out again. Later more titles were added.

More than half the employees who took books home said their children often preferred reading aloud to watching television.

One borrower said, "The minute I get in the door it's 'Read to me, read to me, Daddy.'"

"We do more reading now," another man agreed. "I get as much kick out of this as the kids."

These comments point to the fact that reading aloud can help children develop a taste for reading, and give pleasure to the parents as well.

Although four- and five-year-olds still enjoy their favorite nursery rhymes, they are ready for longer stories. They like to help choose the book. Their likes and dislikes are positive and in a state of transition.

I shall never forget the book I gave Peter when he was four. As I read it to him, I realized that I had bought hastily and unwisely on the strength of stunning pictures. The text was wretchedly dull. Peter listened with a polite show of interest to the end. Then he quietly closed the book and said, "Let's put it in the trash basket." And he did.

This boy had already developed critical taste in reading. While he listened, he was learning to think and evaluate. I am sure this was the result of his parents' skill in reading aloud and discussing with him what they had read. But they weren't trying to be teachers. Their reading and their talk were for pleasure.

In that household read-aloud time is the high point of Peter's day and a sacred hour. As bedtime approaches, Peter collects the books he wants to take upstairs. Sometimes his father or mother will bring another volume. The dinner dishes wait, and so does television. Visitors can join the story hour or shift for themselves.

The read-aloud time is relaxing because everyone knows it will not be interrupted. It is stimulating because Peter's mother and father put life and sparkle into the way they read. It is never dull because they borrow from the public library the best books they can find and they purchase books that Peter will enjoy.

Finally, the reading is successful because Peter is a participant from beginning to end. Besides choosing the books, he often recites memorized lines from his old favorites. Sometimes he makes up his own words for the pictures. He helps hold the book and, if he wants to turn back to a certain picture, he turns back.

Because of this first-class performance by his parents, Peter is growing up with the feeling that reading and books are vital.

The sound of words gives special pleasure to children of this age. Perhaps that is one reason why they like books by Dr. Suess, which have many rhyming words with new twists.

Books for the Fours and Fives

Almost all the books suggested for younger children are well loved by the four- and five-year-olds. (See pages 14 to 19.) Nursery rhymes and tales are still popular and new ones will be learned eagerly. Now the child will take pride in reciting an entire Mother Goose rhyme or retelling a favorite nursery story.

ANIMAL STORIES are very popular with four- and five-year-olds. These children like stories about cats, dogs and horses, but they are ready to hear about the less familiar animals too, such as camels, lions, monkeys and elephants.

Theodore Turtle, by Ellen MacGregor, is the amusing story of one who forgets where he leaves things. On his way upstairs to find one possession, he leaves another behind—and so it goes.

Horton Hatches the Egg, by Dr. Seuss, is about an elephant who is so kind he sits on the nest of Mayzie the lazy bird, hatching her egg.

Anatole, by Eve Titus, is the gay story of a mouse

I had a little baboon and I put it in a boat
I had a little luck and it turned into . . .

From I had a little . . . , *by Norma Levarie, illustrated by John Wright (Random House)*

who commutes by bicycle to a big cheese factory where he is the chief taster. The pictures by Paul Galdone are fascinating.

Caps for Sale, by Esphyr Slobodkina, provides hilarious confusion. A cap peddler takes a nap under a tree. When he wakes up, his caps have disappeared. He looks up in the tree and sees countless monkeys, each wearing a cap and grinning.

The Happy Lion, by Louise Fatio, is a French lion who leaves the zoo to see the world. But wherever he goes his old friends and admirers run from him. Finally the zookeeper's son recognizes him and leads him back to the zoo.

Flip, by Wesley Dennis, tells of a lovable colt who is afraid to jump a stream. He dreams he has wings and flies across. Then he finds the actual jump easy. Small children see Flip's hesitation as a reflection of their own.

I had a little . . . , by Norma Levarie, although not a story, delights children from the first guessing rhyme:

> *I had a little minnow and I put it in a pail*
> *I had a little luck and it turned into . . .*
> *a whale.*

Each turn of the page brings another chance to guess the animal and a new surprise. The pictures by John Wright are intriguing.

THE CHILD'S OWN WORLD always attracts attention. Four- and five-year-olds like stories and pictures about the things they see around them and about other children like themselves.

"Hi, Mister Robin!" and **White Snow, Bright Snow,** by Alvin Tresselt, describe the seasons in delightful text with pictures by Roger Duvoisin.

The Snowy Day, written and illustrated by Ezra Jack

Keats, shows the quiet fun of a small boy's adventures one snowy day.

Switch on the Night, by Ray Bradbury, and **While Susie Sleeps,** by Nina Schneider, help explain the mystery of night. In the first of these a little boy discovers that the dark is friendly, even funny.

A Little House of Your Own, by Beatrice Schenk de Regniers, shows the many places where a small child has his own secret house.

Grandfather and I, by Helen E. Buckley, is a small boy's happy appraisal of his grandfather's unhurried ways and his protest against the frenzied rush of everybody else.

A Friend Is Someone Who Likes You, by Joan Walsh Anglund, is a tiny book that is warm and tender.

STORIES ABOUT MACHINES, TRAINS AND PLANES are much enjoyed by four- and five-year-olds who are quick to recognize various automobiles and types of planes. All sorts of machines—bulldozers, road scrapers, hoists—appeal to them.

Little Auto, Little Train and **Little Airplane,** by Lois Lenski, are among the simplest. Each tells of the popular Mr. Small and his adventures.

Mike Mulligan and His Steam Shovel, by Virginia Lee Burton, seems much more advanced and is a favorite. Mary Anne, the steam shovel, proves to be Mike's best friend and digs her way to a happy ending.

Little Toot, by Hardie Gramatky, is about a playful tugboat in New York harbor who spurns responsibility until a time of crisis.

The Big Book of Real Building and Wrecking Machines, by George J. Zaffo, gives interesting information and stunning pictures that young children follow eagerly.

More and more young children are asking about submarines and space ships. One three-year-old brought a submarine book for me to look at and discuss with him. His questions were about the diving equipment and submarine controls.

Don't be surprised if your three-year-old turns from **The Three Bears** to a book about astronauts. Remember this is a mark of our times.

Many of the books suggested for six- and seven-year-olds—even ten-year-olds—appeal to younger children as well. (See also the general list in Part IV.)

They Like Books of Their Own

By the time a child is four or five, he is beginning to be quite possessive. He wants to call some books his own.

If he has a place to keep his books, he takes more pride in adding new ones. He will welcome books as presents. He will also welcome some of the books that you had and loved as a child. (Suggestions for helping the child build his own library are given in Chapter 14.)

If you have a good public library in your community, you are fortunate. By the time your youngster is four or five, take him to the children's room and show him the picture books. Help him select one or two; then find a chair and low table where he can see the pictures and turn the pages easily.

Remember, the library is a strange world to a child at first, so don't hurry. Children like to drink in new experiences at their own pace.

If the library has a story hour for your child's age, talk it over with him and plan to go. Frequently a program is arranged for waiting parents. In any case, get acquainted with the children's librarian. She can suggest suitable stories and books and may have useful book lists.

Whenever you visit the library, alone or with your

youngster, explore the books for children. Bring home several for read-aloud time. If the child can help in making the choice, so much the better.

A visit to your local bookstore can provide the same delight to a child. Take him in occasionally so that he can see the books and perhaps assist in making a purchase. (See also Chapter 15, "Buying Books for Children.")

3.

When He Starts to School

It's a big step when a child starts to school. To him it is proof that he is growing up. He's really on his own.

Some children take this great step when they enter nursery school at three or four. Others begin with kindergarten at five. Both nursery school and kindergarten are apt to be informal and homelike, with a great deal of playtime.*

Where kindergarten is part of the same school system, the step to first grade is an easy one. Still the child may find quite a difference between kindergarten and first grade. If he hasn't attended kindergarten, first grade may seem overwhelming.

The First Day of School

We generally tell a child about his first day at school long before it comes. As older children begin school, we remind the younger one that his turn will come next year or the year after. During the summer before enrollment, we talk about September. Unfortunately our remarks sometimes cause doubt and anxiety in a child. If we are care-

---

*Helpful information about nursery school and kindergarten is given in *A Parent's Guide to Children's Education,* by Nancy Larrick (Trident Press, $5.95).

Red and Red lived on the same block, but they were not friends.

From The Two Reds, *by Will and Nicolas, illustrated by Nicholas Mordvinoff (Harcourt, Brace & World)*

ful, our reminding can make him look forward to school with pleasure.

For the child who has not been to nursery school or kindergarten, the biggest task may be learning to work and play with others. He has played at home, of course, but in much smaller groups.

You can help him prepare for his first school days by

talking about the things he will do with other children—singing, listening to stories, playing games. You could ask as you read a story, "I wonder if your teacher will read this one?" Talk of this kind will show him that school will have some familiar landmarks.

Most children take the first day in their stride and are ready to tell about it at home. Your questions can make your child feel secure—or produce uneasiness.

If tempted to ask, "Well, what did you learn today?"—don't. The first weeks of first grade are a time for getting acquainted. The child doesn't have specific lessons. He can't tell you what he learned, but he can probably tell about his teacher, the songs they sang and the games they played. After a few days he may want to tell about his school friends.

What about Reading?

Parents are so interested in their children's reading that they often inquire about it prematurely. "Can you say your ABCs?" "Do you have your first primer?" "Have you learned to read yet?" All of these questions seem to demand "Yes" for an answer. The child who has to say "No" may be embarrassed.

The first weeks of first grade are usually a time of *preparation* for reading. Instead of being plunged into book reading, many children go through a carefully planned program to get them ready. Some may not start with books until January or February—sometimes not until the second grade. (See Chapter 12, "How Reading Is Taught Today.")

From the beginning your help is needed. As a start, get acquainted with the teacher. She can tell you about the school program and why things are done a certain way. You can tell her about your child: What is he especially interested in? Why is he a little shy? What are his favorite stories? The teacher needs answers to these questions and many more. Later she will know your child so well that she will be able to give you a new slant or two. The two of you working together can do wonders that could not be accomplished alone.

Once you know the teacher, you will see many ways to help.

✓ *First, show the child you have confidence in him.* Praise him for things well done. Word your questions so they do not seem to be criticisms.

✓ *Show your interest in school life.* Encourage him to talk about the day's events and the people in his school world. But don't insist if he doesn't want to and don't be anxious if he sometimes prefers to keep his home world and school world apart.

✓ *Be sure he is physically fit.* Good food and plenty of sleep are all-important. Watch out for bad tonsils, poor vision, undue fatigue.

✓ *Help him to know other children.* This may be important especially if the teacher reports he is shy at school. A hot-dog picnic in the back yard may build confidence that the child needs in reading aloud.

✓ *Get him accustomed to speaking distinctly* by showing a decided interest in conversation with him. If the two of you join in reciting favorite poems, he may get the feel of talking quickly and easily. (Robert Louis Stevenson, Laura E. Richards and Dorothy Aldis have written some choice poems for this age. More detailed suggestions are given in Chapter 10, "The Power of Poetry.")

✓ *Play listening games* if he enjoys them. They will help him notice likenesses and differences in words he will meet later in print. For example, think of big words made from two little ones, such as *bluebird, buttermilk* and *moonlight;* and words made from basic words like *big* (*bigger* and *biggest*) and *work* (*works, worked, working, worker*).

√ *Answer his questions* about the meaning of words, but don't push him into reading words from a ready-made list.

At this stage one of the most important things you can do is to show that reading is fun. When the child is convinced that stories and books can bring great pleasure, you have made a real contribution.

Fun with Reading

When he enters school, a child may seem to become a different person. He belongs to two worlds—home and school—and he is exploring both for all he's worth. He may try to assert his independence with big talk at home. Yet he still likes to be babied on occasion.

Often his taste in stories is contradictory. At one moment he purrs over some of the old nursery stories and simple folk tales. In the next he demands to hear about rockets and space ships, subjects on which he is surprisingly well informed.

He knows he will soon start reading, and he looks at books with new curiosity. He examines pictures for clues and more than ever wants to know "Why?"

Reading aloud to a six- or seven-year-old is one of the best ways to satisfy his spirit of exploration. The stories he hears at school aren't enough. He needs a regular read-aloud time at home every day.

Being read to at home is different. The child can select the books. He can interrupt whenever he has a question or wants to recite part of the story. And he gets a fine feeling of intimacy because this reading is for him alone.

With a little encouragement the youngster will "read"

a familiar story to you, using the pictures as clues and quoting the simple text from memory. This is the time to use a rebus edition of **The Little Red Hen,** with pictures substituted for certain words. After reading the story aloud several times, you will find you can pause at each picture, and the child will happily supply the word.

By this time children are digging a bit deeper into the stories they hear. As four- or five-year-olds they simply accepted the facts in **The Story about Ping.** A duck got lost and found its way back. Now the listeners want to know why the ducks went back to a boat every night. And why was the boy tied to the boat with a rope? Could he swim? What kept him floating? Why do the boats look so funny?

These are the questions we hope a child will ask when he reads by himself. If he looks behind words and pictures now, he is moving toward independent reading. But don't try to make the child ask questions or to answer yours. This kind of pressure can kill the joy of reading.

Taking a book to school is one way to increase a child's pride in book ownership. Many teachers ask each child to bring something to show and explain to the class. A book is an excellent choice for a show-and-tell period.

Magazines whet the curiosity of six- and seven-year-olds. **Life** and **Look** attract them. **Humpty Dumpty's Magazine,** a monthly for young children, has stories, puzzles, rhymes and games. (See page 272 for address and subscription rate.)

Visiting the public library to select books and enjoy the story hour will give the child a sample of the good things in store for him. Regular visits will persuade him that a library is as important as a gas station or a shopping center.

Increasing the child's own stock of books will build his pride in reading. Grandmothers, aunts and family friends will be pleased to know about wanted books.

Good Books to Read Aloud

At this age children are eager to try all kinds and sizes of books. Many of the titles listed for the fours and fives will be welcome, and there is a wealth of beautiful books designed for six- and seven-year-olds.

ANIMAL STORIES continue to be very popular, particularly those with humor or deep-rooted sentiment.

The Biggest Bear, by Lynd Ward, tells of a small boy who brings home a bear cub that grows and grows and grows. A typical picture shows the little boy in one end of his boat and the biggest bear in the other.

Billy and Blaze, by Clarence W. Anderson, is a touching story of a boy and his loyalty to his pony. Their adventures are continued in **Blaze and the Forest Fire,** and **Blaze and the Gypsies**—all popular with sixes and sevens.

The Two Reds, by Will and Nicolas, pictures the adventures of a boy and a cat in a big city. The story is told with simple text and bold illustrations.

FUNNY STORIES are constantly requested. To children of this age exaggeration is always funny, and repetition makes it funnier.

The Duchess Bakes a Cake, by Virginia Kahl, tells of a noblewoman who makes a cake so light that it raises her high in the sky. There seems no way to rescue her until she calls down to her friends and family: "I'll start eating down; you start eating up."

Andy and the Lion, by James Daugherty, is another favorite. Andy had read so much about lions that when he met one he befriended it—and was suitably rewarded.

The Five Chinese Brothers, by Claire Huchet Bishop, is an old folk tale retold with illustrations by Kurt Wiese.

Because of their remarkable powers—one could swallow the sea, one could not be burned, another could hold his breath indefinitely—the brothers save themselves from catastrophe.

The 500 Hats of Bartholomew Cubbins, by Dr. Seuss, is uproariously funny to children. Bartholomew is puzzled when the King commands him to remove his hat because his hat is in his hand. But he reaches up and finds another—which is replaced by another and still another, while the King threatens the poor fellow with death.

CHILDREN'S ADVENTURES are fine for six- and seven-year-olds who identify themselves with the leading characters.

Especially good is **The Bears on Hemlock Mountain,** by Alice Dalgliesh. Eight-year-old Jonathan is sent over the mountain to borrow an iron pot. On the way he

The Fifth Chinese Brother was shovelled into the oven.

From The Five Chinese Brothers, *by Claire Huchet Bishop and Kurt Wiese, illustrated by Kurt Wiese (Coward-McCann, Inc.)*

keeps saying, "There are no bears on Hemlock Mountain. There are no bears on Hemlock Mountain." But as darkness falls, he hears sounds that prove there *are* bears. Quickly he hides under the iron pot until he is rescued. The simplicity, the suspense and the rhythm of this story make it ideal for reading aloud.

Lentil, by Robert McCloskey, is about a boy, his harmonica and his struggle to become a real musician. By practicing in the bathtub, Lentil is sure the sound is improved 100 per cent.

Madeline, by Ludwig Bemelmans, has become a classic as a book and as a movie. Madeline goes to boarding school in Paris. When she is hospitalized with appendicitis, all the other little girls want to join her.

Popular stand-bys on the adventure list are the **Betsy** books and the **Little Eddie** books by Carolyn Haywood. Little Eddie launches big projects that end in embarrassing or amusing situations. Both series give warm pictures of family and school life.

Down, Down the Mountain, by Ellis Credle, tells of two Blue Ridge Mountain children who want squeaky shoes more than anything in the world. They raise turnips and take the crop to town to exchange for shoes.

Fantasy and whimsy are also enjoyed by six- and seven-year-olds.

My Father's Dragon, by Ruth Stiles Gannett, tells how Elmer Elevator, armed to the teeth with bubble gum, rescues a dragon from captivity and makes a lifelong friend.

Many Moons, by James Thurber, is about a little princess who wanted the moon. Her father, the King, ordered one person after another to bring it to her. The surprise ending shows how it can be done.

Georgie, by Robert Bright, is the story of a gentle little ghost who arouses a family every night by stepping on a loose board on the stair and pushing a squeaky door.

INFORMATION, particularly about science, is eagerly sought by youngsters even before they can read. Librarians report that first graders ask for books about radiation, electronics and outer space. Many spend hours poring over photographs and diagrams in space books written for twelve-year-olds.

You Will Go to the Moon, by Mae and Ira Freeman, and **A Book of Moon Rockets for You,** by Franklyn Branley, give accurate information in the simplest terms with excellent diagrams. Many second graders can read these books.

Books about trains, boats and planes are still very popular. In 1963, one librarian reported, "Sometimes we think trains are far in the lead despite the space age." **The Big Book of Real Trains** and **The Big Book of Real Boats and Ships,** written and illustrated by George J. Zaffo, have many pictures and diagrams with explanatory text that young children enjoy.

Interest in science extends to many areas. Weather, rocks, prehistoric animals, reptiles, insects and the sea are very popular subjects. **All Around You,** by Jeanne Bendick, and **Your Wonderful World of Science,** by Mae and Ira Freeman, are excellent introductory books for the very young science fan.

The True Book of Baby Animals, by Illa Podendorf, intrigues children. **What's Inside?,** by May Garelick, is an exciting series of photographs showing how a baby gosling breaks through the eggshell. The text gives a clear explanation.

While you are reading aloud at home, your child is probably taking his first steps toward independent reading at school. This is all the more reason to continue reading aloud at home. The interest you create will encourage him to keep trying on his own.

4.

As He Begins to Read

In school most children begin to read between the ages of six and six and a half. Many of them complete several preprimers and primers by the end of first grade. Some push ahead faster, and some are slower.

Every child has his own pattern of growth. It determines when he will walk and talk and lose his baby teeth. In somewhat the same way, each child learns to read at his own pace. Sometimes the one who makes a slow start will eventually outstrip his classmates.

Frequently adults forget how long it took them to become independent readers. They want their child to be first in his class. Foolishly they measure his accomplishments against those of the child next door or an older sister who reads like a breeze. They may even make the beginning reader feel ashamed, which is almost sure to slow him down.

If you understand how reading is taught in school, you are in a better position to help at home. (For information turn to Chapter 12, "How Reading Is Taught Today.") To learn about the situation in your child's classroom, talk with the teacher. She can tell you what books, if any, are being used, what progress your youngster is making, and how you can help at this stage.

Someday your child will bring home his primer to read to you. Drop everything to listen. You may hear a tense little voice reading something like this:

Oh, Tom.
Come and look.
Come, Tom, come.
Look. Look. Look.

This is something less than great literature, and the child who regularly uses such words as *astronaut* and *satellite* may also be aware that it's baby stuff. But the crucial fact is that he is reading—not just talking. And the more appreciation he gets from you, the faster he will move out of the "Come, Tom, come" orbit.

The Vocabulary Problem

Nobody knows how many words the first-grade child understands. One estimate is 23,000. Certainly today's child recognizes more words by ear than you did at the same age. Radio and television bring thousands of words into our homes today. The child listening to a weather report may hear *humidity, temperature, barometric pressure* and *wind velocity.* On the TV screen he sees trade names of products while he hears the words pronounced. He may even learn to read them. It is not unusual for a young child to begin reading TV ads at three or four. In conversation he may show that he has picked up a large and grown-up vocabulary.

But the books he meets at school are far from grown-up. The stories are written with the fewest possible words, used over and over for practice. The vocabulary is increased gradually, but it's far behind the child's speaking vocabulary. A first reader can't provide a smashing story because few children can read such difficult words as *astronaut* and *guided missile*. Plots are limited to experiences with such old-fashioned equipment as little red wagons.

Many teachers provide variety by having children dictate their own stories to be read in class. Often such stories tell about pets, holidays and school trips. First-grade teachers report that more and more of these dictated stories deal with exploration in outer space and the threat of war. Given a choice, many of today's children turn to topics we once thought of as adult.

Increasingly, schools are providing library books to supplement the readers. Illustrations and content are generally more attractive than in the average reader.

This is a critical period for a child. He wants to read, but the material he can read himself may not set his soul on fire. His discouragement may lead to a slump unless both parents and teachers are on the alert.

There are at least three ways you can help:

1. *By continuing to read aloud from the most thrilling and the most beautiful stories you can find.*

2. *By guiding the child to books that are easy enough for a beginner to read himself.*

3. *By creating reading materials from the child's experience.*

Creating Reading Materials

One good way to get appropriate reading materials is to make them with the child's help.

√ *Signs and labels* are splendid for beginners. You can make a sign for a bridge or a railroad yard built of blocks. You can label each row of vegetables in the garden. You can label the child's possessions. In the bedroom of a seven-year-old girl I once counted seven different signs: "Doll House," "Doll Dresses," "My Books," and so on.

Children like to make, or help make, signs of this kind. They will read them aloud for visitors.

√ *Experience chart* is the term the teacher uses for a story which a child dictates to read himself. It is so named because it tells of the child's own experiences. If the teacher is using experience charts, you may wish to try them at home.

A good place to begin is with the child's report about something important to him. It may be only a phrase that you remember, but write it down and read it back to him. Show him that these words are his—they say just what he said.

Perhaps he has seen a dog fight on his way from school and comes bursting in to tell you about it. After the first excitement, suggest a story about it. As he dictates, write the words on a large sheet of paper. (Dull-finish shelf paper is fine.) Then read the story together.

Here is a story dictated by a six-year-old who was just beginning to read:

Our Trip to the Farm

Today it was sunny.
We went to the farm.
We saw a truck and a tractor.
Tom rode the truck.
I rode the tractor.

After he had dictated his story, the youngster read it with genuine pride. A few days later he wanted to dictate another, and then another. Sometimes he went back to his early stories to read them again.

If you do record such stories, use the manuscript writing which is customary in the early grades. This is the way the letters are formed:

abcdefghijklmn

opqrstuvwxyz

Make the letters child-size: at least an inch high.

These letters are very much like the printing a child sees in books—yet they have the same basic form as the cursive writing of adults.

Manuscript writing is easier and quicker for a child's fingers. It is usually a good basis for cursive writing which he will begin in grade three or four. Here are the two easy steps from manuscript writing to cursive writing:

Manuscript writing	The step between	Cursive writing
can mile	can mile	can mile

Experience charts are easy to make and extremely useful when a child is learning to read. When he dictates a story, he watches as his words go on paper. When he returns to the paper, he knows that the printed letters will give back to him his exact words and ideas. He sees that reading is communication: from him to the paper, from the paper to him.

A variation of the experience chart is the letter that goes to a relative or friend. This letter was dictated by a six-year-old:

My little bus has silver lights.

I got new gray clay. And it's my clay. I play with it on the bed.

Yesterday we played train and I was the engine and Beverly and Grace and Mary were the cars. But Beverly is the coal car.

I have fun playing with my little red bus. I can write

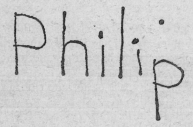

Of course the child cannot read his letter again once it goes into the mails. But he can look for an answer, thus discovering a pleasure that we hope will last a lifetime.

Books for Beginning Readers

Finding books for beginning readers is far from easy. Some books which look simple use long sentences that make reading difficult. Some of those labeled for beginners are really more suitable for second graders. There are almost no books for the child who is just learning to read.

The teacher and librarian can tell you about favorite books for the child who has had some practice with experience charts and a primer—books which are easy and at the same time genuinely appealing. Detailed comments on 330 such books are given in **Books for Beginning Readers,** by Elizabeth Guilfoile. (Published by the National Council of Teachers of English, 508 S. 6th Street, Champaign, Illinois. $1.)

As you explore the library and book stores, you will soon note certain marks of the easy-to-read book:

- The type is large and clear.
- The vocabulary is simple, and sentences are short (sometimes only four or five words).
- Lines are short with the line break coming where you ordinarily pause in conversation. Example:
  No one has been
  to the moon.
- There are only a few lines on each page.
- Pages are uncluttered, and white space is plentiful.
- The pictures give clues that make reading easier.

When the lines rhyme, the child may get a hint that helps identify new words. When there is repetition, he may gain assurance and so quicken his pace.

As you read one of these simple stories aloud, you will find it is more pleasing if the words flow smoothly and rhythmically. Children respond to language that sings, even when it is read at their slow pace.

They know what they want to read about, too, and it is usually not the subject matter found in their pre-primers and primers. One survey of first graders showed that only 3.3% selected library books about other children and their parents—yet 94% of the material in their pre-primers and primers was about children and their parents. About one child in a hundred chose to read about toys, but in the preprimers and primers over 28% of the material dealt with playthings.

COMICAL SITUATIONS appeal to almost all children. Whether it is gentle humor or slapstick comedy, they read it over and over.

One of the funniest stories for beginners is **The Cat in the Hat,** by Dr. Seuss, which tells about the pranks of a cat that comes to visit on a rainy day. Thanks to its rhyme and simple vocabulary (223 different words), this story can be read by many children at the end of the first grade.

Are You My Mother?, by P. D. Eastman, has a vocabulary of only 100 words. This story of a baby bird in search of its mother has gentle humor. My own copy has been worn to shreds by neighborhood borrowers.

"I guess there is no place for me to hide," cried the dinosaur.

From Danny and the Dinosaur, *written and illustrated by* Syd Hoff *(Harper & Row)*

Danny and the Dinosaur, by Syd Hoff, tells of a small boy and a museum dinosaur on the town for a day. The dinosaur tries to hide in a game of hide-and-seek.

Fierce John, by Edward Fenton, is about a little boy who pretends to be a lion. His family out-pretends him.

New scenes and adventures are always welcomed by young children. They are presented beautifully in **Indian Two Feet and His Horse,** written with only 130 different words by Margaret Friskey. The little Indian who is told to use his own two feet goes out and finds a horse for himself. The pictures suggest the art of the Plains Indians.

Look Out for Pirates!, by Iris Vinton (177 words), is a more grown-up tale of shipwreck, a box of gold, deep-sea diving, and pirates who are bombed out by a hornets' nest. It is easy reading for second and third graders.

A warm personal appeal makes some books especially popular with children. Such a book is **I Know a Farm** (177 words) by Ethel Collier, in which a little girl explores a farmer's barn all by herself. Her discoveries make the reader feel he is part of her adventure.

Little Bear, by Else Holmelund Minarik, is a gentle story with an old-fashioned look. But Little Bear has won a devoted following of modern children who enjoy his birthday party, his trip to the moon, and the continued adventures in **Father Bear Comes Home, Little Bear's Friend** and **Little Bear's Visit.**

Nobody Listens to Andrew, by Elizabeth Guilfoile, is about a little boy with momentous news, who is shushed by everybody until inadvertently his news leaks through. Hasn't every child been in this predicament?

Informational books on this easy level are less plentiful than storybooks, but they are increasing. Children go for them. If they can't read the text, they pore over the pictures.

The **Let's Find Out** books by Martha and Charles

Shapp (about 100 words each), and the **I Want To Be** books, by Carla Greene (under 200 words), are among the simplest. **Let's Find Out About Electricity** and **Let's Find Out What's Light and What's Heavy** are very popular. **I Want To Be a Scientist** gives a good introduction that children welcome.

You Will Go to the Moon, by Mae and Ira Freeman, and **The Moon Seems to Change,** by Franklyn M. Branley, answer persistent questions of six- and seven-year-olds.

Seeds and More Seeds, by Millicent E. Selsam, combines a slight story with information. The suggestions for seed experiments make this very popular.

Even in the early grades, children are quite selective. What appeals to one may not appeal to another. And the book you choose may not be the one the child wants. Children vary. Even more baffling is the fact that a child may take **Little Bear** to his heart one week and demand a book about pirates or space ships the next.

The way you introduce a book may influence the reception it gets. If possible, give the child a hand in selecting the book at the library or bookstore.

At first it may be a good plan to read the book aloud, with the child following, page by page. After one or two readings, he may be ready to read whole sections to you or even the entire book.

Don't worry if a child's first reading is simply reciting from memory. (Children do that so easily that they sometimes fool their elders.) When a child follows the printed words he repeats from memory, he is getting good practice in associating spoken word with printed word—which is the basis for all reading.

When a child hesitates over a word, read it for him promptly so he can move ahead. Don't ask him to sound out letters and syllables at this early stage lest you create confusion and mar his budding pleasure. Above all, don't make a list of words for drill.

Your role at this beginning stage is to show that reading can be a pleasure and that books can bring delight. If your co-reader shows signs of restlessness, respect his right to choose another book or move on to something entirely different. If it is understood that the two of you will help each other with reading, with plenty of time to talk about pictures in between, this kind of shared reading will help him move from the role of listener to performer.

Keep On Reading Aloud

Although the child in first, second and third grade can read simple things alone, his choices are limited. He reads in a halting fashion that makes the best story sound dull. This is one more good reason why you should continue reading aloud even though he is beginning to read independently. The swinging vigor of your reading will give him a model. And the colorful language in stories too difficult for him to read will remind him of treasures ahead.

Read him some of the simple books that he will soon read himself. But be sure also to read some of the wonderful books he may not be able to read for several years.

By all means, consider these possibilities:

Chanticleer and the Fox, retold and illustrated by Barbara Cooney—a book with everything: a good story, exquisite illustrations, suspense, humor and a happy ending.

Houses from the Sea and **The Day We Saw the Sun Come Up,** by Alice E. Goudey, beautiful picture books with interesting information for children.

Going Barefoot, by Aileen Fisher, the poetic story of

a little boy longing to go barefoot who watches the tracks of rabbits and raccoons, squirrels and mice as he waits for the Barefoot Moon in June.

Crictor, by Tomi Ungerer, the story of a boa constrictor which becomes the pet and friend of an elderly school teacher.

From Crictor, *written and illustrated by Tomi Ungerer (Harper & Row)*

A Hole in the Tree, by Jean George, the story of a hole in an apple tree which begins as the tiny hole of a bark beetle and grows until it is big enough for a raccoon.

The Happy Orpheline, by Natalie Savage Carlson, the lively adventures of 20 little French orphans, continued in **A Brother for the Orphelines.**

Fun with Oral Language

When the child is beginning to read, he is trying to match sounds with print and with meaning. He will do this more easily if he speaks clearly and easily. One way to help him with reading, then, is to encourage him to talk freely.

Give a sympathetic ear when he reports on his doings. Bring him into family conversations when you can. Ask him about his experiences at school, about the television programs he has seen and the playtime adventures he has had.

WORD GAMES continue to interest youngsters at this age and are valuable in developing reading skill. "Categories" is an old favorite. A category is chosen (flowers or four-legged animals or baseball players, for example). Then each person names as many words as he can for the category. The game can be played orally without pencil and paper.

"How Many Syllables?" is a popular listening game. Explain how to count syllables. Then see how many two-syllable words the group can name, how many three-syllable words, and so on. A variation is to announce a word and ask each player to raise two, three, or four fingers for the number of syllables. Such games can make children sensitive to the various sounds in familiar words.

STORYTELLING GAMES are another useful resource. You can begin one elementary type with a simple statement: "Once upon a time there was a little boy named Bill." Then it is the child's turn to tell the next part of the story, as, "Bill had two puppies. One was black and one was brown." Now you figure out what the next sentence might be.

In the game "Who Am I?" one player pretends he is a storybook character. He gives a few clues to help the guessers. For example, "I am a rabbit. I hid in a watering can." The child who guesses "Peter Rabbit" becomes the next pretender.

It Takes Time

Too often parents become critical when their child begins to read. Sometimes they expect a second- or third-grade youngster to read flawlessly. Instead, he reads one word after another with equal emphasis and no change of pitch. He doesn't talk like that—why does he read like that? And sometimes he makes the same mistake over and over. Shouldn't he be drilled on the words he misses?

Go to the teacher if you have questions like these. She knows how your child is getting along. She may tell you he needs more informal practice in reading aloud.

You can do a great deal at this important stage by encouraging the child to read aloud and by reading to him from interesting books. From these two-way experiences he will discover new satisfaction in reading.

5.

When He's On His Own in Reading

It's usually in the third grade or early fourth that a youngster finds his stride in reading. Then he needs little outside help, and he enjoys his independence.

Some children have an insatiable appetite for books in this period. They vie with each other in the number of books read, sometimes reading a book a day. They explore new subjects and new kinds of stories. Often they go back to an old favorite and reread it four or five times. They choose easy books and more advanced ones, occasionally dipping into adult titles.

Frequently, though, a slack period follows in which the once-avid reader avoids books altogether. Parents should not be discouraged by this reading slump, for the youngster is likely to begin reading again when he finds a subject, a hobby or the kind of book that appeals to him.

Some children may not become eager readers until the fifth or sixth grade, and still others will never read anything they don't have to read. Often these are the ones with strong scientific or practical interests who would rather build something than read about it. The fact that they never become eager readers is no cause for alarm. They can read when they have to.

In short—as every observant parent knows—children differ from one another. It will help to remember that a child can succeed even if he doesn't love to read.

Nine to Twelve, the Vigorous Age

Children of nine to twelve have boundless energy and great endurance. Boys will work for days to build a racing car or perfect a system for sending messages to the friend next door.

It is a time when youngsters begin to feel very grown-up and independent. Each youngster is likely to have a best friend with whom he does everything, including sharing and exchanging books.

Above everything, children want the approval of boys and girls their own age. Everything must be done the way other children do it, and woe betide the parent who tries to buck this need for group approval. Neighborhood clubs are springing up. Each club shows remarkable uniformity in haircuts, socks, books and almost everything else. Youngsters are active in church clubs, Boy Scouts, Girl Scouts, Boys' Clubs, Camp Fire Girls and 4-H Clubs. The programs of these national organizations give excellent guidance for local reading activity.

Age nine usually marks the height of the TV and comic-book craze. By ten the two interests are subsiding. (See Chapter 7, "What about the Comics?" and Chapter 8, "Television and Children's Reading.")

For children of this age the world is rapidly expanding beyond home and school. They are experimenting with new interests and hobbies. Some of them will have seven or eight different collections under way at one time. They like to identify and classify: "What kind of rock is this? Can it be called a sedimentary rock?"

They are constantly challenging. "How come?" and "How do you know?" test the good humor of parents every day. Yet these questions are heartening for they show eagerness to reason things out and verify information. Both are good leads to reading.

Reading Lessons at School

Although the pupil in the upper elementary grades can read independently, reading lessons at school are being continued to extend and sharpen his skills. By now he is writing more stories and reports, so he must polish up his handwriting and become a good speller. His work in spelling is giving him a better sense of syllable division, and that helps with reading.

His teacher is showing him how to tackle new words in print. He is becoming more skilled at silent reading, too, and he is learning to speed up his reading for certain purposes. He begins to know when to skim and when to read carefully.

His tendency to raise questions and verify information helps him evaluate what he reads. What does the author mean? How does he know? Thus the child learns to become a critical reader.

After the third grade children are reading more about science, history and other subjects. Textbooks may be harder to read than storybooks because they use unfamiliar terms and compress a great deal of information into a short space.

Sometimes the young reader must figure out special meanings for old words. For example, in reading of prehistoric times, he may come to the term "land bridge," describing a stretch of land that once joined Asia and North America and it served as a bridge for prehistoric animals. This is probably a new idea to the child.

His curiosity makes him a ready user of the dictionary, the almanac and the encyclopedia. At school he is being introduced to reference books and is learning when and how to use them. Further practice at home will be helpful. (For suggestions, see Chapter 9, "Let's Look It Up!")

Perhaps you wonder how well your child is using his new reading skills. One teacher has listed four test questions:

1. Does he voluntarily turn to reading for information and pleasure?
2. Does he find material related to things he is interested in?
3. Does he try to help himself with his reading?
4. Is he beginning to vary his manner of reading according to the material and his reasons for reading it?

If the answer is yes for each question, you can be sure he is making progress. Whether the answer is yes or no, there are many ways in which you can help him develop greater pleasure—and hence greater skill—in reading.

Your Example Is Important

Children are imitative. They are more likely to seek out books if they grow up in a home where adults turn to books. If you read, your children will probably read, too.

If you buy books, they know that books are important to an adult. If you borrow regularly from the library, your children will soon have cards.

Of course, not all parents are confirmed readers and book lovers. Unless you grew up enjoying books, you may feel that a book is the last thing you want after a hard day's work. Even so, you can help establish a child's positive attitude toward reading. For example:

• Take time to read aloud to your nine-, ten- and eleven-year-olds and have them read aloud to you. (Many of their books will prove refreshing reading for adults as well.)

• Encourage them to talk about the books they have been reading or want to read.

- Use their questions, their interests and their hobbies as leads to choosing reference books and further reading of all kinds.
- Be sure there is a comfortable place and a good light for reading.
- See that there are good books from which the youngster can choose—at the school library, the public library and in your growing home library.

Your appreciation of reading as one doorway to a good life will show in the way you speak of books and the time you devote to your child's interest in reading. It won't help to label one member of your family a bookworm while exalting the Little Leaguer who never reads.

Children's Interests Lead to Reading

The nine- to twelve-year-olds are full of interests. They seek new hobbies, new sports, new friends. They like trips and expeditions. Inspecting a house under construction appeals to many children. Exploring a shopping center will satisfy others. An over-night camping trip in the mountains will thrill almost any youngster of this age.

All these interests can lead to reading, if you help to make the connection and provide the reading material. For every hobby there are related books—attractive books telling how to collect butterflies or perform magic tricks or play baseball. And for every question, big or little, there is an authoritative answer in a dictionary, encyclopedia, almanac or other book. For every trip there are road maps and timetables to help in planning—and all require a special kind of reading. There are field guides to help in identifying rocks and reptiles, or sea shells and marine plants. The historical tour can lead to related informational books and stories.

The step to reading is more likely to take place if you guide deftly. When questions are raised in daily conversation, turn to a dictionary or encyclopedia for the answer. Before the next family trip, let your ten-year-old study the road map and chart the course. (Map reading is one of his big assignments in social studies at school.) In baseball season, find a baseball story or the biography of a baseball hero. For further suggestions, turn to Chapter 6, "When He's Interested, Nothing Can Stop Him."

Television can become a springboard to reading, provided children learn to question what they see and to seek more about the TV story. Chapter 8, "Television and Children's Reading," suggests ways to convert these interests into good reading.

Surround Him with Books

Almost everyone reads more when he is surrounded with tempting books. Children are no exception. The modern classroom displays books face out to attract the reader. All the youngster needs to do is reach out and help himself. He doesn't have to ask permission or sign up formally. The teacher doesn't have to argue or coerce children to read; attractive books sell themselves.

Many parents are using the same technique. One mother writes, "All this winter we have tried to surround Jerry with books. We got books from the library—the exciting books the librarian suggested—and just put them in places where Jerry was bound to see them. We didn't push him to read, but he couldn't help seeing these books. Now he is reading them and having fun at it."

Your most valuable role may be to show your youngster how to get what he wants from the library. Help him find the section which has books for his reading level. Then give him plenty of time to browse and sample. Pick some books for yourself and for the younger children while he is making his choices. But don't hurry—the thoughtful reader needs time to decide on a book. Librarians tell me that parents who take plenty of time to select their own books sometimes expect their children to decide in thirty seconds.

Before visiting the library, talk about the kind of book the youngster might like to borrow. An animal story? A mystery? Another book by Beverly Cleary? The book that the boy next door recommends?

The teacher, the school librarian and the public librarian can all suggest books that your child is likely to enjoy. The book lists described in Chapter 16 will help too.

Frequently children make lists of recommended books at school and use them as a guide. In one school in Virginia, each class makes a monthly list of books recommended by the children themselves. The lists are sent home for posting in some prominent place "such as over the kitchen sink." One mother commented, "This meant I was putting books on my grocery list. Now we go to the library every time we go to the supermarket. We're all reading."

Books Children Choose Today

Sometimes parents expect their children to like the same books they liked. And often they do. **Little Women, The Adventures of Tom Sawyer, Heidi** and **The Wizard of Oz** rank high on any list of children's favorites.

But some of the books you remember may be slow going for today's children. Or you may have forgotten when you read a certain book and try to introduce it too early. Before you try to pass on a book from your childhood, read it again with your child in mind.

Books that get off to a fast start are especially popular today. Perhaps this is because children are used to immediate action on television. If a program does not please them at once, they try another. In a book, they like some sign that things are under way.

In **Charlotte's Web**, E. B. White arrests his reader with the first line: "Where's Papa going with that ax?" Anybody would want to find out.

From The Horse Without a Head, *by Paul Berna, illustrated by Richard Kennedy (Pantheon Books, Inc.)*

In **The Horse Without a Head,** Paul Berna opens with this paragraph:

Gaby and the rest of the gang were there in front of Fernand Douin's house at the top of Poverty Lane. One after another the ten children mounted their horse and shot down the hill at top speed to the Street of the Black Cow at the bottom. There the rider jumped to the ground and ran back up the slope dragging his steed behind him to where his friends were impatiently waiting their turn.

With that start, children keep reading.

Here is the beginning of William O. Steele's **Winter Danger:**

> "There's a hollow sycamore 'round the bend," Jared Amis yelled to his son. "We'll hole up there for the night."
>
> Micajah Amis nodded. There was no use trying to make his pa hear him over the drumming of the rain and the roar of the swollen creek beside them. Besides there was nothing to say, though Caje reckoned a hollow sycamore was the last place in creation he wanted to sleep. He might as well be a 'coon or a 'possum.

When you select a book for a child, look for action in the first two or three paragraphs.

HISTORICAL STORIES appeal to many children because they are full of action. Youngsters like to read about mutiny in a covered wagon train, the threat of Indian raids, wolves stalking the cattle, and the specter of starvation. Davy Crockett and Wyatt Earp may have set the pace on television. Certainly children remain devoted followers of the wild frontier.

One of the easiest historical stories to read is **Riding the Pony Express,** by Clyde Robert Bulla. The hero is the son of a Pony Express rider who has to pinch-hit for his father on a harrowing ride. Even third graders can read this one.

Another popular story is **The Matchlock Gun,** by

Walter D. Edmonds. It tells of a young boy who fires an old matchlock gun during an Indian raid in which his mother is hit by a tomahawk.

Many stories show that pioneer families, for all their hardships, had a great deal of fun. Such a book is **Caddie Woodlawn,** by Carol Ryrie Brink. Caddie, a tomboy, lived with her family in Wisconsin when Indians still threatened.

The Pony Express, by Samuel Hopkins Adams, and **Custer's Last Stand,** by Quentin Reynolds, are popular informational books with the vigorous action that the nine-to-twelves want.

Many biographies have a strong appeal. One is **Carry On, Mr. Bowditch,** by Jean Lee Latham, the amazing story of a boy who mastered the art of navigation and became a famous mariner. James Daugherty's **Daniel Boone** has hair-raising adventures and a homespun quality. Both of these are for advanced readers in the upper grades.

Better readers in the sixth grade will thrill over **Calico Captive,** by Elizabeth George Speare, which recounts the adventures of a girl captured with her family in an Indian raid in 1754.

STORIES WITH WELL SUSTAINED SUSPENSE are always first choices, although the plots may be extremely simple.

One thrilling story is **Call It Courage,** by Armstrong Sperry. Young Mafatu, son of a Polynesian chief, is marooned on an island inhabited by cannibals. By making his own weapons and canoe, he escapes and becomes a hero.

One of the most gripping books is **The House of Sixty Fathers,** by Meindert DeJong. A Chinese boy is separated from his family in wartime and makes a heroic effort to find them. The boy's devotion to his pet pig and the almost terrifying suspense make this one of the most exciting recent stories for eleven- and twelve-year-olds.

ANIMAL STORIES with a strong line of suspense have almost universal appeal.

Along Came a Dog, by Meindert DeJong, is such a story. It is about the strange and wonderful friendship between a homeless dog and a little red hen.

Lassie Come-Home, by Eric Knight, is the classic story of a dog who traveled hundreds of miles to get home again. Countless children have wept happily through this book, only to go back and read it again.

A stray dog is the hero of **Old Yeller,** by Fred Gipson, a thrilling and heart-breaking story voted "my favorite book" by thousands of children. Old Yeller is a cattle dog in the Texas hill country of the 1860s.

Horse stories are especially popular with girls in this age group. One ten-year-old told the librarian: "I like to read everything so long as it is about horses." She listed her favorites: **The Black Stallion, The Black Stallion and Satan** and **The Island Stallion.** All are by Walter Farley.

The horse stories of Marguerite Henry are also extremely popular. Among her best are **King of the Wind, Misty of Chincoteague** and **Sea Star.** Although **King of the Wind** has won more honors, **Misty of Chincoteague** is the sure favorite of fourth- and fifth-grade girls. Misty, a wild pony, is caught in the annual roundup and tamed by two youngsters. The story is moving and beautiful.

Also at the top of the list is **Old Bones, the Wonder Horse,** by Mildred Mastin Pace. This is a rags-to-riches story of a horse that came out of nowhere to win the Kentucky Derby.

HUMOROUS STORIES are always popular with the nine-to-twelves.

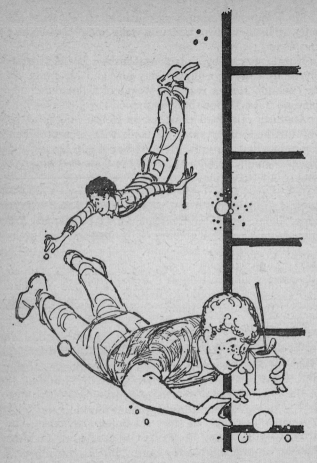

The two boys quickly learned how to handle themselves in the absence of gravity.

From Danny Dunn and the Anti-Gravity Paint, *by Jay Williams and Raymond Abrashkin, illustrated by Ezra Jack Keats (McGraw-Hill Book Co.)*

Mr. Popper's Penguins, by Richard and Florence Atwater, tells how two penguins take over the Popper household.

Homer Price, by Robert McCloskey, is the irresistibly funny story of a present-day boy and his gang. On one occasion Homer is left in charge of a doughnut machine he doesn't know how to stop.

Another well-loved character is Henry Huggins, the typical American boy, who contends with such problems as guppies that multiply too fast. The series by Beverly Cleary includes **Henry Huggins, Henry and Beezus, Henry and Ribsy** and many more.

Equally popular is Danny Dunn, the junior scientist whose fantastic inventions are reported by Jay Williams and Raymond Abrashkin in **Danny Dunn and the Homework Machine, Danny Dunn and the Anti-Gravity Paint** and so on.

An excellent story is **The Enormous Egg,** which Oliver Butterworth tells in the words of 12-year-old Nate Twitchell, the owner of a living dinosaur that is investigated by the House Un-American Activities Committee.

Ellen MacGregor's stories about Miss Pickerell are very popular. This precise lady whisks off on startling expeditions that are hilarious. For example, **Miss Pickerell Goes to Mars** and **Miss Pickerell Goes to the Arctic.**

The same kind of dead-pan humor stamps the tall tales which children love. **When the Mississippi Was Wild,** by LeGrand, explains serious facts quite unseriously. The partial taming of the Mississippi is attributed to Mike Fink, a champion fighter. He battled Old Al, the alligator, and tied his tail halfway to prevent him from raising more than a half-tail storm. **Cap'n Dow and the Hole in the Doughnut** is a great favorite by the same author.

BOOKS IN SERIES enjoy a bull market with children of this

age, who are already collectors of everything from match folders to coins.

The term *series* has many meanings. Generally it means a number of books by the same author about the same characters. The **Betsy** books and **Little Eddie** books of Carolyn Haywood are popular with eight- and nine-year-olds. Walter R. Brooks has made a juvenile hero out of Freddy, a pig on the Bean Farm who suffers from a tragic handicap—he has practically no tail to curl. The series includes **Freddy the Detective, Freddy Goes to Florida, Freddy and the Space Ship, Freddy the Cowboy** and many more. Freddy fans wouldn't dream of missing a single title.

A family chronicle is another kind of series, with each book covering a different period. Examples are **The Moffats, The Middle Moffat,** and **Rufus M.,** by Eleanor Estes, and Elizabeth Enright's stories about the Melendys: **The Saturdays, The Four-Story Mistake** and **Then There Were Five.**

Girls especially are devoted to the Laura Ingalls Wilder chronicle that begins with **Little House in the Big Woods,** followed by **Little House on the Prairie, Farmer Boy, On the Banks of Plum Creek** and **By the Shores of Silver Lake.** Little Laura in these stories is the author, telling about her own childhood on the edge of the big woods in Wisconsin almost eighty years ago.

Occasionally a series consists of books by different authors on different subjects, issued by one publisher under a series name. The North Star Books, the First Books, the Landmark Books, and the Allabout Books are often called series books. All of these are informational, not stories.

The identifying names of these series add to their appeal. Librarians report that children who try one of the I Can Read Books or First Books come back to ask for another. Occasionally I meet youngsters who proudly say they have read every Landmark Book. They seem to feel this is an achievment like owning a complete set of hard-to-find stamps.

There is no doubt that reading a series is like pursuing a hobby. The more you do it, the more you like it, until the interest subsides and you are ready for a new subject.

How can a child read so many *Freddy* books? Won't he ever get tired of that pig? Don't worry. One of these days he will wake up to discover that literature is even broader than pigs.

Some books in series are beautifully written and attractively illustrated. Some are superficial and repetitious. Within a series of informational books, some books are much better than others. Your help will be needed in avoiding the shallow fiction and the misleading nonfiction that may be published in series.

FANTASY, I find, brings mixed response from children. Many are real fantasy fans. One librarian reports: "We can't keep up with the demand for this type of story. 'I want a book about witches,' the children say. Or, 'about dragons,' as the case may be. We cannot keep enough copies of Anna Elizabeth Bennett's **Little Witch** on our shelves."

A Bear Called Paddington, by Michael Bond, has endeared itself to seven- and eight-year-olds who sympathize with Paddington's talent for getting into trouble.

The Magician's Nephew and **The Last Battle,** two of the Narnia stories by C. L. Lewis, are moving experiences for the right child.

There are children whose first inclination is to spurn a story of magic, wee creatures, even talking animals. They may tell you they don't like stories that couldn't really happen.

But often the same children enjoy **Mr. Popper's Penguins** and thrill over the impossible achievements of scientist Danny Dunn. They follow Miss Pickerell in book after book. There is a great deal of realism in these books of fantasy, and the unreal situations create humor which children enjoy. This is also true of **The Magic Chalk,** by Zinken Hopp, in which a school boy finds a piece of magic chalk and draws a pal who comes to life. Together they draw their way in and out of fabulous adventures.

In many cases, fanciful stories need a special introduction. When a child hears a chapter or two read aloud, he is apt to want more of the same.

The Cricket in Times Square, by George Selden, is such a story. Once a child meets the musical cricket from Connecticut and his friends—the fast-talking Broadway mouse, Harry the Cat and Mario the newsboy—he is eager to hear more. The scene is in a New York subway station, often a hard-hearted world, but also the place where Chester the Cricket finds friendship and beauty. Fanciful as it is, **The Cricket in Times Square** enjoys the benefit of setting, characters and conversation that are familiar to many children.

The Borrowers and **The Borrowers Afield,** by Mary Norton, are English stories that tell of little people who live by borrowing all the tiny objects you thought had been lost—a gold safety pin, a few beads or jewels, the top of the aspirin bottle. The Borrowers must keep out of sight of mortals so they live in secret nooks furnished with borrowed items. These books and their sequels are also wonderful to read aloud.

INFORMATIONAL BOOKS are read eagerly by boys and girls in the upper elementary grades.

Nature and science are particularly popular. There is great demand for books that tell of prehistoric times—about the first animals, early men, cave paintings, and so on. Good examples in this field are **Dinosaurs,** by Herbert

S. Zim; **All About Dinosaurs,** by Roy Chapman Andrews; **The First Book of Prehistoric Animals,** by Alice Dickinson; **Before and After Dinosaurs,** by Lois and Louis Darling; and **Prehistoric World,** by Carroll Lane Fenton.

The attraction of books about space travel and the universe is very great. Both girls and boys read eagerly such books as **Off Into Space,** by Margaret O. Hyde; **Exploring Mars,** by Roy Gallant; **All About the Planets,** by Patricia Lauber; **Junior Science Book of Stars,** by Phoebe Crosby; **The Earth Satellite,** by John Lewellen; and **Project Mercury,** by Charles Coombs.

Books about the sea, especially underwater exploration, seem to be growing in popularity. Those about rocks and the earth's changing surface have a big following.

Fortunately there are many well written children's books which give authoritative information with excellent illustrations about almost every aspect of science—mammals, reptiles, insects, minerals, plant life, weather, electricity, heat and sound, for example.

Factual books about the people and events of history are also well liked by the nine- to twelve-year-olds. Almost any book about World War II seems to win a following. **The Diary of a Young Girl,** by Anne Frank, is very popular with sixth and seventh graders as are **Thirty Seconds Over Tokyo,** by Bob Considine and Ted Lawson, and **The Sinking of the Bismarck,** by William L. Shirer.

Books about the opening of the American West are popular too, perhaps because they include realistic details of hardships and extreme danger.

Real interest in biography is likely to develop in this period. Children are curious about important individuals, past and present. While they want to know about the childhood and youth of the greats, they usually prefer the whole life story.

Some of the best-liked informational books for children are described in Chapter 6, "When He's Interested, Nothing Can Stop Him," and in the annotated list at the end of this book.

Shall We Read Aloud to Children Who Can Read Independently?

Yes, by all means! They love it.

But shouldn't they be reading for themselves now that they can? Won't it spoil them to read to them?

Of course they should be reading to themselves. But they should have the fun of being read to as well. Furthermore, read-aloud time is ideal for introducing new books.

A child likes to sample before he reads. In the library he will dip into one book after another before he makes a choice. Sometimes those samples are all too brief, and the decision goes against the book for that reason.

But if several chapters are read aloud at home, he gets into the meat of the book. Also, the very sound of your voice may add the life and spark that will put it over.

Some books—like cherished friends—grow on you slowly. It would be too bad to miss these gems simply because they were introduced too hurriedly.

The human voice does a great deal to endear a story to the listener. Characters come alive when their conversation is actually spoken. Of course reading aloud cannot turn a poor story into a good one. Indeed, one reliable test of a book is to read it aloud. If the language is awkward, the rhythm jerky, and the dialogue unnatural, these defects are more obvious than in silent reading.

The fanciful stories that make the impossible seem possible are excellent for reading aloud. Once I presented **Charlotte's Web,** by E. B. White, to a nine-year-old boy who asked if he could bring in "the kid next door" to lis-

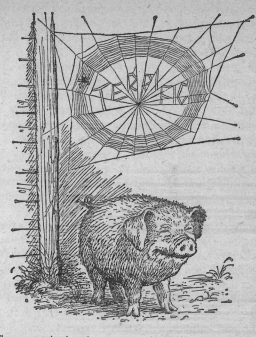

There was the handsome pig and over him, woven neatly in block letters, was the word TERRIFIC.

From Charlotte's Web, *by E. B. White, illustrated by Garth Williams (Harper & Row)*

ten while I read aloud. When the neighbor showed up, I had qualms. These were two rugged lads who might scorn a book about a web-writing spider and an undersized pig. But as I read, they slipped into the relaxed posture and faint smile that showed interest. We read three chapters before dinner, and they made me promise to finish the book on subsequent evenings. Now, several years later, when I go back to visit, Miss Charlotte A. Cavatica is still talked about with real affection. She is certainly the most lovable spider of all time.

The Wind in the Willows, by Kenneth Grahame, is equally suited for reading aloud. It reports the adventures of four old friends—Mole, Water Rat, Badger and Toad—who live along the Thames below Oxford. They dress, dine, and converse like English country gentlemen at the turn of the century. Their dignified discourse is very amusing when read aloud. And the exquisite descriptions of the woods and riverbanks take on fresh color and depth. Although many children will not start this book by themselves, almost every youngster gets a glow of pleasure from listening.

Legends and folk tales are ideal for reading aloud, perhaps because they have come down to us from ancient storytellers who knew just how to paint a vivid picture in rhythmical language. I think all ages will enjoy the French Canadian folk tales in **The Golden Phoenix,** by Marius Barbeau, as well as **The King's Drum and Other African Stories,** by Harold Courlander.

Virginia Haviland's series of **Favorite Fairy Tales— Told in Germany, Told in Ireland, Told in Russia, Told in Norway,** etc., will furnish evening after evening of delightful reading aloud. These books are so simply written that many fourth graders—even some third graders—can read them alone.

Poetry is welcomed by the nine-to-twelves, too. In fact, children of all ages enjoy it—once they hear it. Because there are no separate age groups for poetry, I have put all the poetry suggestions into Chapter 10, "The Power of Poetry."

There is no doubt that a child of any age loves to be read to. I think, too, that adults get immense satisfaction from sharing favorite stories and poems. I have read to so

"Come along, Red-comb," said the don-key. "We're going to Bremen."

From Favorite Fairy Tales Told in Germany, *retold by Virginia Haviland, illustrated by Susanne Suba (Little, Brown & Co.)*

many children that I find myself thinking of one book or another in the way some child has responded to it. When I read new ones, I classify them according to the responses I think they will get.

The best books and poems belong, of course, to all ages. Adults like them almost as much as children do.

The humor of Dr. Seuss in **And to Think That I Saw It on Mulberry Street** is for you as well as for your child. The adult reader may be laughing at one level and the child at a different one—but both are laughing.

In **The Wind in the Willows** the adult may see humor in the grave remarks of the conceited Toad that the child misses, but the child may respond more readily to the ridiculous scrapes Toad gets into.

In a family with several children, read-aloud time may be one of the few occasions for family gatherings. Older children will be pleased to introduce their favorites to the younger ones. They may take a turn at reading aloud. The younger children will feel honored to listen to these more grown-up stories.

Old and young delight in hearing Kipling's **Just So Stories.** Try reading "The Elephant's Child," which begins: "In the High and Far-Off Times the Elephant, O Best Beloved, had no trunk." When the Kolokolo Bird says, "Go to the banks of the great grey-green, greasy Limpopo River, all set about with fever-trees, and find out," we go.

This kind of reading aloud will provide a warm feeling of family unity that will be cherished through the years.

6.

When He's Interested, Nothing Can Stop Him

Teachers, librarians and parents used to list the books every child should know. The aim was to get the child interested in each one.

Now we realize it is better to begin with the child and the things he cares about and then find the books that suit him.

Almost every child has some driving interest. It may be his dog or baseball or coin collecting—or even comic books. At play, children may become so absorbed in a project that they actually forget about eating.

The same driving force can be directed to reading, provided the child finds the right books. The second grader who is fascinated by dinosaurs may read half a dozen books about them. His enthusiasm may push him to read third- and fourth-grade books which might otherwise have seemed too hard.

One eight-year-old who collected snakes spurned reading until his third-grade teacher suggested **All About Snakes,** by Bessie M. Hecht. A new world opened up. David read and read. By the end of the year his reading level had jumped three grades.

Most children are bubbling over with interests—nonliterary in most cases, but vigorous and absorbing. The younger ones are popping with questions, too—some of them asking for simple facts, others probing into cause and effect.

Obviously this is one way to introduce books and reading. If you can learn what a child is most concerned with, what he is dreaming about, it is easy to find a book to fit.

Discovering His Interests

Some children are very outspoken about their interests. Others are quite reserved. A child may develop an interest at school and not mention it at home. Or he may have a slight interest that can be strengthened with a little encouragement.

If you know what attracts your child, you can find books that will attract him equally. Discovering his inclinations is not always easy, for they may change from week to week—and the range is almost unlimited. But if he is sure you are a sympathetic listener, he is likely to speak out. You might compare notes with his teacher, who may have a line on interests and ambitions you have not discovered.

Often a few casual questions will get revealing answers from a child: If you could do the thing you most want to do, what would it be? If we could take a one-day trip, where would you go? If we could live in another country or in another age, what would be your choice? If you had a museum of your own, what would you put in it?

Or, turn the conversation to "one thing I wonder about." When a children's magazine invited its readers to write on "One Thing I Wonder About," the editor got more than 6,300 replies. Almost half of the questions were about science or nature. Some of the wonderings:

I wonder where the stars go during the day.
How can a baby lamb know which one is its mother?

Why does the moon change its shape?

What's at the bottom of the ocean?

How can the earth be round and yet people don't fall off?

I wonder how the birds find their way back from the South.

How come an island can keep on floating?

Each of those questions leads naturally to reading. Each would prompt the thoughtful parent to produce an appropriate book.

When nine-year-old Lucy came to visit us in the country, her one desire was to ride a pony. Fortunately, pony rides could be had at the Farmers' Market, and Lucy had plenty. "Here's a story about a horse," I said later, pulling out **Plug-Horse Derby,** by Emma L. Brock. It is the story of a little girl who trains her entry for a plowhorse derby and wins. From this Lucy went to **The Blind Colt,** by Glen Rounds, and **Blue Canyon Horse,** by Ann Nolan Clark, the poetic story of a little mare who deserts an Indian boy to enjoy the freedom of the wild. Lucy's love of horses spurred her on.

Developing New Interests

Childhood is the time for sampling and exploring. Even the youngest have questions. By encouraging the questions, we encourage more exploring and the building of new interests. There is no better way to stimulate reading.

Wherever you live, you are surrounded with the stuff that questions are made of. The weather is a good example. Where does rain come from? How did it get into the clouds? What is snow? What is fog? Can you make a cloud in your kitchen? Why are the days longer in summer? Why is it colder in winter?

These simple questions are extremely interesting to children. They lead to other questions too—questions about the wind and air currents and gravity, for example. Easy science experiments can be set up to explain simple facts about the weather.

All these questions and activities lead to reading. And a number of books fit this interest beautifully.

The Storm Book, by Charlotte Zolotow, is for the youngest—a charming picture book about the beauties of an approaching storm. My own **Junior Science Book of Rain, Hail, Sleet and Snow** is simple enough for many second graders to read on their own. More advanced readers will enjoy **Exploring the Weather,** by Roy Gallant, and **Thunder and Lightning,** by Herbert S. Zim.

HOLIDAYS—which we often take for granted—can be the start of questions and lead to reading, too. In the midst of Halloween excitement, read **Tell Me, Mr. Owl,** by Doris Van Liew Foster, to your five- or six-year-old. For the family read-aloud hour, choose from **Ghosts and Goblins,** a wonderful collection of stories and poems, edited by Wilhelmina Harper. Or read Margaret Embry's **The Blue-Nosed Witch,** the story of Blanche, a friendly witch who joined some trick-or-treaters on their neighborhood rounds.

At Christmas, there is a wealth of stories and poems to read aloud or to recommend for children to read themselves. **Told Under the Christmas Tree** is a lovely collection of stories and poems for Christmas and Hanukkah. Another is **The Animals' Christmas,** edited by Anne Thaxter Eaton. For fourth and fifth graders learning about United States history at school, **Christmas on the Mayflower,** by Wilma Pitchford Hays, is a thrilling story with the true meaning of Christmas shining through. **The Light at Tern Rock,** by Julia Sauer, tells of a memorable

Christmas holiday when a boy and his aunt are stranded at a lighthouse.

Stories and poems related to our most important holidays and religious celebrations are included in **Holiday Storybook,** edited by the Child Study Association.

HOBBIES, too, may be a lead to further interests and further reading. Most children from six to twelve are riding at least one hobby, whether it is collecting baseball cards or playing a trumpet. Some hobbies last only a few weeks or a few days; others are enjoyed for months or years. Either way, the observant parent can build on them.

Stamp collecting, for example, is a natural approach to geography and history. It is a hobby that can last for years, and books will make it even more interesting.

The child who collects bottle tops or match folders may be gaining very little from this activity. But his love of collecting and his skill in gathering, sorting, and storing might be diverted to a more worth-while hobby if he knew the possibilities.

For example, collecting insects is an exciting hobby that relates outdoor fun to reading. What is the large reddish-brown butterfly with black and white markings? The field guide identifies it as a monarch. At the library the child finds **Monarch Butterfly,** by Marion W. Marcher, and **Insects in Their World,** by Su Zan Noguchi Swain. There are many natural history books for children which are scientifically accurate, well written and handsomely illustrated.

How-to-do-it hobbies absorb many youngsters: how to cook, how to build or make something, how to be a ballet dancer, how to take pictures, how to perform magic tricks. Often they require special materials or special lessons. They can be leads to reading, too.

For girls interested in ballet there are many fine books. **Fun with Ballet,** by Mae Blacker Freeman, gives directions and photographs for each ballet lesson. **Ballet for Mary,** by Emma L. Brock, and **Ballet Shoes,** by Noel Streatfeild, are stories about enthusiastic students of the ballet.

Sports are the hobbies of many children, and here again we have books to make the hobby more interesting. For third and fourth graders, Beman Lord has written several fine sports stories, notably **Quarterback's Aim** and **Guards for Matt. How Baseball Began in Brooklyn,** by LeGrand, is a tongue-in-cheek explanation that children love.

Young magicians will be helped by **Fun With Magic,** by Joseph Leeming, and **The First Book of Magic,** by Edward Stoddard.

OUTINGS AND TRIPS stir new interests. It does not need to be a big or expensive trip. What the child wants is to see new things and get new ideas. A little child will be satisfied with a walk in new-fallen snow. His older brother may choose a trip to the swamp beside an abandoned railroad, or a visit to the junk yard.

To some people a swamp is simply muck; but to others it is an exciting world of plants, insects and animals. And to the child with a mechanical turn, the junk yard can open vast fields of interest. An old automobile battery or parts of an engine may excite one explorer as much as the other is moved by marsh marigolds. And in both areas—nature and machinery—there are endless questions to be pursued.

The nine-to-twelves prefer an all-day trip and are eager to help with preparations. Is there a state park in your area? A historic shrine? A factory that welcomes visitors? Invite the youngsters to work out a good route on the road map. They might write for literature about the place to be visited.

One mother told me that her nine-year-old sends for

Many a snake helps the farmer by devouring rats and mice.

From All About Snakes, *by Bessie M. Hecht, illustrated by Rudolf Freund (Random House)*

road maps in advance of a trip. He and his father choose the route. Along the way the boy jots down interesting facts or questions about places to be looked up when he gets home. "They are the questions we all want answered but usually forget," the mother added. "Besides, they get us all reading."

Any trip can offer exciting leads to nature and science—provided the driver is willing to pull off the road and stop from time to time, or explore an unpaved side road. Carry in the glove compartment several of the **Golden Nature Guides,** such as **Birds, Flowers** and **Trees.** For a dollar each gives you 160 pages (paperbound) with full-color illustrations, range maps, identifying data, and an index. These guides can be used by youngsters in the fifth grade and will be interesting to the entire family. At home have a copy of Margaret Waring Buck's **In Woods and Fields,** which pictures and describes plants and animals you are likely to meet in various settings and seasons. Older children will enjoy **The Tale of a Pond** and **The Tale of a Meadow,** by Henry B. Kane, who recounts his experiences with good text, photographs and drawings.

If you have had a day at the seashore, round out its pleasures by reading **Houses from the Sea,** with beautifully poetic text by Alice E. Goudey and exquisite sea shell illustrations by Adrienne Adams. For older children, **See Along the Shore,** by Millicent Selsam, has an excellent section on shell fish, with beautiful illustrations by Leonard Weisgard.

Perhaps your trip raises questions about rocks and how they were formed. You may have brought home a number of interesting specimens. If so, you have an ideal introduction to any of the good books about rocks, including **Junior Science Book of Rock Collecting,** by Phoebe Crosby; **The First Book of Stones,** by M. B. Cormack; and **Rocks, Rivers and the Changing Earth,** by Herman and Nina Schneider.

Family outings can lead to similar investigations of history. As a beginning, take time to read historical markers. Usually they give just enough information to raise further questions. Why was this battle important? What was this area like one hundred years ago? You will find many children's books about historical events and personalities as well as about particular areas.

In the Pennsylvania German area where I am living, I find countless things to stir my curiosity. What is the meaning of the geometrical symbols painted on old barns? Who are the people wearing the plain clothes that suggest the Pilgrims' costumes? What are the strange words that we find on the restaurant menu? Questions like these are answered in three good stories by Marguerite de Angeli: **Henner's Lydia, Skippack School** and **Yonie Wondernose,** which describe the customs and folklore of the Pennsylvania Germans. Many of the author's illustrations repeat the quaint painted decorations of early settlers in Pennsylvania.

Colonial Williamsburg, the Mississippi, New England, the Southwest, the Northwest, and many other regions are well presented in books for children.

PEOPLE can lead to reading too. Children are always meeting interesting people: a new child in school, a new family down the street, a new hero on TV. All can be the source of new interests and new reading.

New neighbors make children wonder about the place they came from. If it was a foreign country, count yourself lucky. Their language, customs and interests can be the path to absorbing books and stories about other lands.

An uncle or older brother on duty in a distant country can prompt interest in finding out more than his letters tell. Or the advent of a foreign car on your block may induce your ten-year-old to read about automobiles.

Indeed, every waking hour is chock-full of people and events and things that can lead a child to a book. Your big job is to help your child meet each day with curiosity and a wish to find out more.

Don't be afraid to raise questions you can't answer. Most adults are very hazy on science, geography and history. Indeed, this very lack of information is a good reason to say, "Let's look it up." Looking it up will give the child experience in using the almanac, dictionary and encyclopedia. (See Chapter 9, "Let's Look It Up!")

To find books related to your child's questions and interests, consult the book lists described in Chapter 16, "Book Lists Aid Selection."

7.

What about the Comics?

In 1962, thirty million comic books were sold in this country each month as against seventy million a month in 1953. (The drop has been attributed to increased TV viewing and paperback book buying.) Each comic book is said to circulate to three readers.

Children who read the comics include the very bright who make good grades and the slow ones who have poor records at school. There seems to be little relation between comics and scholastic standing.

For years comic books have been a source of worry and complaint among parents. They have even been investigated by Congress. Since 1960, however, the critics have eased their attack on comic books and turned to television.

Why Worry about Them?

Comic books vary greatly. Some are picture stories about funny animals and people in funny situations. Some give information on subjects close to boys' interests. At the other extreme are the adventure stories, murder mysteries and thrillers. In these you often find violence, terror and sheer horror.

Several years ago the crime comics were so violent

that many parents protested. Some critics blamed the publications for contributing to juvenile delinquency. In self-defense, many comic-book publishers banded together to enforce better standards. (You may have seen comic books bearing the seal of approval of the Comic Code Authority.)

However, there are still some comic books which are filled with terror and sensationalism. One which I purchased in 1963 at the Philadelphia Airport tells of a drug addict who invades a hospital operating room with a switch-blade knife, threatening to slash the patient's oxygen line. Threats, physical violence, gunfire and critical injury follow in rapid succession. Since this terror-laden story bore the title of a mass-audience TV program, it may have had millions of readers.

Even the improved comics would hardly be a parent's first choice for his child's reading. The paper is cheap, the colors garish, the drawings harsh. To me the books are ugly, but I must admit that some youngsters react quite differently.

The literary content is equally disappointing. A story is told in jerky snatches of conversation, blurted out with little or no explanation of inner feelings and thoughts. Nowhere do we find the fine descriptions of people and places that prevail in a good book.

Comic books based on the classics are so condensed that the original story seems a gaudy skeleton, sometimes badly distorted.

Yet a child may spend hours with the comics—hours that might be devoted to worth-while reading or wholesome outdoor activities. When will he move on to books that will challenge his intelligence and touch his heart? Much will depend upon the sympathetic guidance he gets from his parents and teachers and upon the good books which are available.

Why Do Children Read the Comics?

There are at least six reasons why children read and treasure comic books. If you understand the reasons, you will be better able to cope with the problem.

1. *The comics satisfy a child's desire for action and adventure.* Even the harmless, funny comics have smash-ups and wild chases galore.
2. *Events move swiftly and episodes are short.* This means quick, almost breathless satisfaction.
3. *They are easy to read.* In fact, a nonreader can often get the story from the pictures.
4. *They are available in every community.* Comic books are sold for twelve and twenty-five cents at drugstores, newsstands, and the five-and-ten.
5. *Other children are doing it.* Boys and girls want group approval. The child who doesn't read comic books may feel he is isolating himself from other children.
6. *Many children have nothing else to read.* They turn to the comics either without knowing there are better and equally exciting books or without knowing where to get them.

"Jimmy never reads comic books," his mother told me emphatically. "I never let the children bring them into my house." The day before I had noticed Jimmy trading comics with another boy on the playground.

The attempt to ban all comic books from a child's life may force him to read them under cover and thus resort to deception. Instead, it may be better to take an occasional look at the comic books your child is reading. If you find one that is filled with crime and violence, explain your reaction to him. Then help him find other reading matter or other entertainment to replace the rejected comic book.

Substitutes for the Comics

Probably the most successful procedure is to introduce the child to books that will be substitutes for the comics. This means careful planning and perhaps some experimenting. But it will be worth doing.

Remember that children find it easy to get comic books. It will be important, therefore, to have better books where the child can get them easily—both at home and at school.

Because comics are abundant, a child is used to choosing from a great number. Similarly he should have a quantity of good books to choose from. He is used to choosing. He expects it.

He is also used to storytelling pictures. He will respond to books with illustrations that tell much of the story.

Many of the books you introduce should be so short they can be read at one sitting. Longer ones may exhaust the interest of a child accustomed to quickies.

Don't forget that the comic-book devotee is used to reading for fun. No one ordered him to read the comics; no one asked him for a report. He will find more fun in other books if he can approach them the same way.

Before introducing good reading, find out what kind of comic books your child prefers. Children under eight often choose the funny ones, including animal comics. Those from ten to twelve are inclined toward comic books of adventure and suspense. Once you know the child's taste, find as many good books in that field as you can.

For some children the books listed below have proved

Pippi wiggled her toes for a while so that the water splashed around everywhere.

From Pippi Longstocking, *by Astrid Lindgren, illustrated by Louis S. Glanzman (The Viking Press)*

good substitutes for the comics. You will find more information about each of them in the annotated book lists beginning on page 205.

FUNNY ANIMAL STORIES

The Cat in the Hat, by Dr. Seuss
Horton Hatches the Egg, by Dr. Seuss
Anatole, by Eve Titus
Curious George, by H. A. Rey
Crictor, by Tomi Ungerer
The Horse Who Lived Upstairs, by Phyllis McGinley
Space Cat, by Ruthven Todd
Mr. Popper's Penguins, by Richard and Florence Atwater

CHILDREN'S ADVENTURES

Augustus and the River, by LeGrand
Pippi Longstocking, by Astrid Lindgren
Lentil, by Robert McCloskey
Henry Huggins, by Beverly Cleary
Homer Price, by Robert McCloskey
The Enormous Egg, by Oliver Butterworth

JOKES, RIDDLES, AND NONSENSE, UNLIMITED

I Met a Man, by John Ciardi
Book of Nonsense, by Edward Lear
What Do You Say, Dear?, by Sesyle Joslin
Yours Till Niagara Falls, edited by Lillian Morrison

STORIES OF DANGER AND SUSPENSE

Custer's Last Stand, by Quentin Reynolds
Winter Danger, by William O. Steele
The Matchlock Gun, by Walter D. Edmonds
The Pony Express, by Samuel Hopkins Adams
Along Came a Dog, by Meindert DeJong
Five Boys in a Cave, by Richard Church
Old Yeller, by Fred Gipson

Take a Tip from the Comics

For the comic-book fan, reading has been easy, exciting and full of suspense. And he has had the additional pleasure of doing what other children are doing.

If the child is to understand that a book is fun, he should get that idea at the start. What he thinks may depend on the way you introduce the new books. Your offerings will not be welcome if you say, "Here are some books you ought to read," or "This will be ten times as good for you as a comic book."

One of the best ways to get him interested is to read part of the book out loud or tell a little about it. If it is a book you have read and enjoyed, your recommendation will have greater effect.

With several children in your audience, you may be able to develop group approval for better reading. I know of one mother who cannily began her better-reading campaign one afternoon when her son and two of his friends were marooned at her house by rain. When she suggested reading aloud **The Enormous Egg,** by Oliver Butterworth, the boys were skeptical. But the humor and suspense of the story quickly showed them that this book was too good to walk out on. By the end of the afternoon one of the boys asked to borrow the book. Unlike the comics, *The Enormous Egg* has so much rich detail in the text that it is interesting on a second or even third reading.

All of these boys had been steady readers of comics. When they began with real books, they continued to read the comics, but only by fits and starts. Gradually they outgrew the craze as they increased their other reading.

This was possible only because good books, appealing books, were all around them.

8.

Television and Children's Reading

When Davy Crockett became a TV hero in 1955, adults were debating a new best seller, **Why Johnny Can't Read,** by Rudolf Flesch.

The children gave the answer to Dr. Flesch. Within a few days of the first Davy Crockett show, they turned to libraries and bookstores across the country and borrowed or bought almost every Davy Crockett book on the shelves. Library waiting lists grew while the first comers read everything they could get their hands on.

Nothing was said about books or reading on the Davy Crockett program. Nobody told the children to read. But they knew what books they wanted.

Other TV heroes have sent children to libraries and bookstores on the double. Wyatt Earp was one example. Robin Hood was another. The television performances of **Peter Pan, The Wizard of Oz** and **Cinderella** created an immediate book demand by the children.

In addition, librarians report that children come to them daily with TV questions. "Do you have a book about astronauts? I saw the news program on television last night." Or: "Do you have a book about nurses and hospitals? That's what I like best on TV."

When a first grader asked for a book about radiation not long ago, his school librarian swallowed hard. "On television they keep talking about it," the youngster explained.

Children of all ages have learned that television can be a natural lead to reading. Of the youngsters questioned in a 1958 survey, 45 per cent believed they were reading more since TV had become a daily habit; 29 per cent less; 26 per cent the same amount. (A few years later almost no American children could remember life without television.) Librarians generally report that children are reading more than ever.

Time for TV and Time for Reading

At the age of three an American child is usually a regular television viewer, watching forty-five minutes a day. In the primary grades he probably spends two and a half to three hours a day watching television. By sixth or seventh grade the average child's viewing time reaches three or four hours daily.

Between the ages of three and sixteen, he will probably spend more time watching television than attending school. At least, this is true of the *average* American child, according to recent research. There are children who spend as much as five or six hours a day before the flickering screen.

With so much time for television, how does a child have time to read?

Researchers tell us that most children have not let television cut into the time formerly allotted to reading books and magazines. But it has cut into time previously given to radio, movies and comic books. Also, it has probably decreased children's time for play.

In general, children in grades six, seven and eight are the heaviest TV viewers. Those in sixth grade include many children of high IQ who are good readers. But by tenth grade most of the high IQ youngsters are no longer heavy viewers. At this stage, it is young people with lower reading ability who spend the most time with TV.

As might be expected, similar television viewing habits are likely to prevail among parents and children in a family. If father and mother watch TV for long hours, the children do too. Frequently adult TV choices are adopted by the boys and girls.

What Children View

The very young child has little to choose from on television except for the animated cartoons. In 1963, there was only one live network program for the nursery school age.

By the time a youngster is in first grade, however, he is probably spending 40 per cent of his viewing time on adult programs. And in one community, sixth graders devoted 79 per cent of their TV time to adult shows.

Adults, on the other hand, are frequently enthusiastic viewers of programs planned for children. "Disneyland" was a classic example. In 1957, it was the overwhelming favorite of children twelve and under. More than two-thirds of those under six watched it frequently, and so did 5,100,000 adults.

The distinction between a children's program and an adult program has become nominal. The Westerns shown in the afternoon and early evening are simpler, perhaps, than those scheduled in what we think of as adult viewing hours, but they are none the less Westerns. Even the crime program, usually thought of as an adult show, is only one step removed from a children's adventure program centering around a super-hero. Both attract children and adults.

As a child dials from one TV channel to another, without plan or purpose, what does he find? Try it for a few

days and see. The choices are likely to include man-
slaughter, drug addiction, mental illness, burglary, ex-
tortion and bitter emotional crises. There are crooked
police, corrupt officials and double-dealers of every kind.
All too often might makes right in the TV world. Even the
milder family dramas may present false values no mother
wants her child to embrace.

According to **America** magazine, 16 per cent of the
TV programs between 4 and 10 p.m. were "crime and
violence shows" in 1954; by 1961 they had risen to 50 per
cent of all programs.

Day and night there is relentless interruption by com-
mercials which glamorize commonplace products. Even
the cartoons for pre-schoolers are shot through with advertising.

Along with the cheap, the sensational and the com-
mercial, there are many entertaining and worth-while
programs. Children need guidance in finding them. They
also need direction in limiting their televiewing so that
they have time for other activities, including reading.

Helping Children Get the Best Out of TV

The younger the child, the more he needs adult help
with television. Random sampling and solitary viewing
by the young child will almost certainly lead to unde-
sirable programs and the possibility of mounting fears
and anxiety.

You can avoid this situation by watching television
with youngsters of pre-school age. If a program is fright-
ening or unhealthy, turn to another channel. Better still,
divert the child's interest to another activity which will
have positive value and which you are willing to share
with him. "Let's take a walk" or "How about making
some cookies?" may be the only inducement he needs. If

you have a good book of stories to read, the promise of another story instead of television may do the trick.

Even with older children, it is important to watch television with them at least occasionally and to be ready with alternate proposals for shared entertainment. Most families set up certain rules to get the best from TV. If children have a voice in making the decisions, compliance will be easier.

A basic rule is to have fixed times for meals and bed. In one family I know, the TV curfew rings at eight with the understanding that reading can go on for another hour. "It's time for bed now," says that mother, "but you can read." With plenty of books to choose from, no one sighs over missing late television.

Similarly, time should be set aside for homework and other responsibilities. Yet the family schedule should be flexible enough to allow for special television programs which may require a change in the routine.

Which programs will be seen within the time limits? Many parents study the week's TV schedule with their children helping in the decisions. A special program like "Alice in Wonderland" will be circled as too good to miss. Your twelve-year-old may insist on a movie on water skiing, while your first choice may be a concert or a baseball game. Once these special programs are scheduled, you can see what else you have time for. As you make your selection, be sure to consider the offerings of your local stations. Some of their children's programs are tops. Also, consult the television recommendations of your newspapers and national magazines.

If you have educational television in your area, watch for the monthly program log. There are now more than seventy educational television stations around the country—about one fourth of the channels reserved for educational use. The daytime programs on most of them are directed to in-school audiences. In the late afternoon there are programs for very young children, in the evening for adults.

Any effort to limit children to educational programs would be doomed. The youngsters are entitled to their quota of excitement. TV viewing can be a good balance between informational programs and entertainment—if it's planned that way. Many of the documentary programs for adult viewers have a strong appeal for ten- and eleven-year-olds.

You can help children develop good taste in TV choices by watching and discussing some programs with them. Ridiculing an inferior program won't help. But a few questions may show the child how to weigh the good and bad points of what he has seen.

You can also help by providing children with other activities and interests. Billions of child-hours are now spent on TV because the children have nothing else to do. When a mother takes time to read aloud or a father helps make toys or the whole family takes off for the country, TV is forgotten.

Children need outdoor play. They need to create things. They want to sing and dance and paint, and do them well. But with so much free entertainment on television they often withdraw to become spectators. Sometimes it is a good thing to watch others perform. TV can introduce new ideas and broaden a child's interests, but the child should be a doer as well as a viewer. With your help television can become a bridge to many creative activities, including reading.

The TV Bridge to Reading

The TV program which dramatizes a particular book is, of course, a direct invitation to reading. After viewing such a program with your youngsters, why not get the book? Then begin reading it aloud. Children who are good readers will continue on their own. When they find out how the story was changed for television, they will debate whether the program was as good as the original book.

Many other programs can be bridges to reading, too. If Westerns are popular in your family, you would do well to introduce the child to some of the books that deal with cowboys and Indians, pioneer life, and the opening of the West. For example: **Riding the Pony Express,** by Clyde Robert Bulla; and for better readers, **The Pony Express,** by Samuel Hopkins Adams. Or **Buffalo Bill,** by Ingri and Edgar d'Aulaire; and **Daniel Boone's Echo,** by William O. Steele.

Cody had such a big armload of wood that he couldn't see where he wanted to go.

From This Boy Cody, *by Leon Wilson, illustrated by Ursula Koering (Franklin Watts, Inc.)*

Television's science experiments, science fiction and science news can be a good introduction to books, too. **One Hundred and One Science Experiments,** by Illa Podendorf, is excellent. For children who like science fiction there are the Danny Dunn and Miss Pickerell books.

Even the weather reports on television relate to children's books, such as **Everyday Weather and How It Works,** by Herman Schneider, or **Lightning and Thunder,** by Herbert S. Zim.

One good technique is to track down books that pertain to a particular television show and read one or more chapters with your children. By 1963 some of the networks were distributing lists of TV-related juvenile books along with announcements of forthcoming children's programs.

The librarian at school or at the public library will be able to suggest titles that tie in with TV. You might also consult the list of children's books at the back of this handbook.

The important thing is to move fast while curiosity and enthusiasm are high. After a while your children will see that books—unlike television—can give depth of information and continuing satisfaction at a pace they can control. The possibilities are unlimited.

Further Reading about Children and Television

Children and TV, by Josette Frank, Director of Children's Books and Mass Media for the Child Study Association of America. An excellent analysis of the situation with practical suggestions for parents. 1962. (Public Affairs Pamphlets, 381 Park Ave. S., New York 16. 25¢.)

Television: How to Use It Wisely With Children, by Josette Frank. An interesting discussion of the good and bad in TV, how various children are affected by it and ways by which parents can make the most of it. 1959. (Child Study Association, 9 E. 89 St., New York 28, N. Y. 25¢.)

Television in the Lives of Our Children, by Wilbur Schramm, Jack Lyle and Edwin B. Parker (Stanford University Press, 1961. 342 p. $6). Fascinating information about the effects of television on children, based on studies of more than 6,000 youngsters.

9.

Let's Look It Up!

It is sometimes embarrassing to admit we have never thought of some of the questions raised by a child. We can rarely give adequate answers, so we must turn to the right book.

A child's questions are cause for rejoicing for they show he is thinking. The best thing you can say is, "Let's look it up." Even if the child reads only a line or two in the dictionary or encyclopedia, he will start a habit that will benefit him for the rest of his life: the habit of going to books for information and satisfaction.

This means you need one or more reference books in your home. There are many kinds that your child can easily learn to use. Those most suited to home use are dictionaries, almanacs, atlases and encyclopedias.

Many Kinds of Dictionaries

Dictionaries are probably the most useful reference books in any home. They vary greatly in size, difficulty, content and price.

A PICTURE DICTIONARY is the simplest. The inexpensive kind sold in the supermarket or chain store entertains the young child who enjoys matching a familiar picture to the given word, but it does little of the work of a real dictionary. More advanced picture dictionaries also include one or two sentences which give the meaning of each word.

The Golden Dictionary, by Ellen Wales Walpole (Golden Press, $2.99), uses more than 1,500 colored pictures with simple sentences to show the meaning. The words are on a rather crowded two-column page.

The Rainbow Dictionary, edited by Wendell W. Wright (World Publishing Co., $4.95), defines 2,300 words through colored pictures, simple definitions and sample sentences. The pages are uncrowded and inviting.

Both books are useful to children in the primary grades. If the child is just beginning to read, the picture will help to identify a new word. Also, he will begin to understand the A-to-Z arrangement of words.

Since a child in the primary grades may know as many as 25,000 words by ear, a picture dictionary is unlikely to introduce any new words. But it may help him become interested in words in print. By third or fourth grade many children are beginning to use a school dictionary.

A SCHOOL DICTIONARY (also called a JUNIOR DICTIONARY) is much longer and more detailed. It shows how each word is divided into syllables, how it is pronounced, what it means (often several meanings) and what part of speech it is. Pictures are included, sometimes maps. Prices range from $3.75 to $4.50.

Six good school dictionaries for elementary children are:

Funk & Wagnalls Standard Junior Dictionary (Funk & Wagnalls Co.). For ages 8-14. 39,000 words.

The New Winston Dictionary for Children (Holt, Rinehart & Winston). For ages 8-12. 32,550 words.

Thorndike-Barnhart Beginning Dictionary (Doubleday & Co.). For ages 8-11. 22,000 words.

Thorndike-Barnhart Junior Dictionary (Doubleday & Co.). For ages 10-14. 43,000 words.

Webster's Elementary Dictionary (G. & C. Merriam Co.). For ages 9-11. 18,000 words.

Webster's New World Dictionary, Elementary Edition (World Publishing Co.). For ages 9-12. 44,000 words.

Each has a good introduction which gives the pronunciation key and explains how to use the dictionary as a whole.

You will note that these dictionaries vary greatly in size from 18,000 to 44,000 words. More important, the content varies. For example:

Webster's Elementary Dictionary does not list proper names of people or places as the others do. The larger the dictionary the greater the list of proper names, of course. The **Thorndike-Barnhart Junior Dictionary** includes a one- or two-inch map with many place names.

Webster's Elementary Dictionary does not give the size of an animal or object beside its picture. Thus, a child, seeing a *jaguar* and a *jay* on the same page, might assume they are the same size because the pictures are the same. Both pictures are easily four times the size of the *jeep* and the *jet plane* shown on the facing page, and the text makes no explanation to the contrary. The other dictionaries give the size (*jaguar, 2½ ft. high at shoulder*) or the ratio of the picture to the real thing (*jaguar 1/20*). Children want that kind of detail.

Many of the words a child is curious about do not appear in some of these school dictionaries. For example, *penicillin, detergent* and *orlon* are in **Webster's New World Dictionary** but not in the other four. Because children do want to know about advanced words, you will find great use for a college dictionary.

A COLLEGE DICTIONARY, written for college students and

other adults, includes around 150,000 entries. Frequently it gives many definitions for a single word. Prices are about $5 or $6.

Four widely used college dictionaries for family reference are:

American College Dictionary (Random House, Inc.).

Funk & Wagnalls New College Standard Dictionary (Funk & Wagnalls Co.).

Webster's Collegiate Dictionary (G. & C. Merriam Co.).

Webster's New World Dictionary of the American Language, College Edition (World Publishing Co.).

These dictionaries are authoritative, well illustrated, and constantly revised to include new material.

In addition to definitions, a college dictionary gives the origin or derivation of a word. Thus it explains that *submarine* comes from two Latin words: *sub* meaning *under* and *marinus* meaning *of the sea*. This kind of information is interesting and important to the curious child.

A college dictionary may be difficult for the child because the type is smaller than he is used to and the vocabulary is more advanced. When several definitions are given for a word, the youngster may have trouble finding the right one. And he is apt to be confused by the abbreviations for the origin of the word and the fields where it has special meaning (for example, *Entomol.*, *Pathol.*, *Zool.*, *Astron.*).

Yet the college dictionary includes information of interest to children in the upper elementary grades. The curious fourth grader hears that penicillin is an *antibiotic*, a word not listed in his school dictionary. The college dictionary has the definition—but in words that are too advanced for most children. The happy solution is to have a school dictionary for the child to use on his own and a college dictionary for you to use with him.

Certainly the more advanced dictionary offers a great deal that is interesting and stimulating to a child.

Many dictionaries not listed in this chapter are sold in drugstores, supermarkets and chain stores, as well as in bookstores. Some are good, some not so good. Before you buy, look up several words you know well and see what you think of the definitions. Are they clear and accurate? Does the dictionary have good illustrations and maps? Is the type legible and clear? Then consult your public librarian or your school librarian. She can give you suggestions and show you dictionaries used in the library.

Learning to Use a Dictionary

If your child is to get the most out of a dictionary, he must understand how to use it. You can help him become acquainted with the distinctive features. First explore the dictionary yourself to find answers to such questions as these:

1. *How is pronunciation indicated?* Usually the key is given at the bottom of each page. But be sure to read the explanation in the front of the book, too. Remember that your dictionary and the school dictionary may have different pronunciation keys.

2. *How is syllable division shown?* Clear divisions will help your child with pronunciation.

3. *How is size indicated on scale drawings?* A 1¼-inch sketch of an otter in the **New Winston Dictionary for Children** is marked "Otter 1/25." This means the animal is 25 times larger than the picture. **The Thorndike-Barnhart Junior Dictionary** labels its picture "Otter (total length 3 to 4 ft.)." Explain to your child what these labels mean.

4. *How is the origin of the word shown* (in a college dictionary)? If you have a college dictionary, help your

young readers to grasp the meaning of the abbreviations that show derivation (such as L for *Latin,* ME for *Middle English,* t. for *taken from,* and g. for *going back to*).

As soon as a child learns to use a dictionary, he has broad resources at his command—resources that will help him with his reading and in dozens of other ways. A parent can easily help a child develop the dictionary habit because there are so many occasions for looking up words at home.

For example, you hear *helicopter* pronounced *heel*-icopter on television. You've been saying *helly*copter. What does the dictionary say? (Most of them say *helly*copter is more commonly used; *heel*icopter is also acceptable.)

At first a child is not likely to question the pronunciation of any adult, let alone a television personage. But he can be shown that skepticism is fun. He can learn how to translate the dictionary's letters and marks into sounds. He will be pleased when he masters this skill. And he will be more alert to pronunciation, including his own.

Maybe you hear Syria mentioned in a news report. But exactly where is Syria? The **Thorndike-Barnhart Junior Dictionary** has a very clear 1½-inch map.

The nicest thing about the dictionary habit is that the worse it gets the better it is.

Almanacs and Atlases

AN ALMANAC is an inexpensive paperback book with hundreds of pages of facts and figures brought up to date annually. By using the detailed index, you can quickly find population figures; names of congressmen and many other officials; biographies of the Presidents; World Series winners for more than fifty years; descriptions of foreign countries; data on the highest mountains, the longest rivers, the highest dams, the fastest trains, the worst shipwrecks—and many thousands of other facts.

Two almanacs most widely used in homes and libraries are:

The Information Please Almanac (Simon & Schuster, $1.50).

The World Almanac and Book of Facts (New York World-Telegram and Sun, paperbound, $1.60).

These almanacs are ideal for getting facts quickly. They contain far more than you would expect to find in a single book. Because they are designed for adults, they have very small type. But today's child of nine to twelve often wants adult information.

AN ATLAS is another reference book which children find interesting as well as useful with school work. Two good ones for children:

First Book Atlas, for grades 3-6 (Franklin Watts, $1.95).

Hammond's Illustrated Atlas for Young America, for grades 5-7 (C. S. Hammond Co., $2.95).

Here again you should take time to show a child how to use the atlas and how to read the maps. Pupils in the upper grades learn these things at school, but repetition at home will help.

For adult use, Rand McNally's **Cosmopolitan World Atlas** ($13.95) is excellent. Older children will enjoy its very detailed maps.

Encyclopedias for Family Use

When a quick, brief answer is needed, an almanac or dictionary may suffice. But when you want more comprehensive information you need a good encyclopedia. It can also serve as a springboard to further reading.

An encyclopedia is a major investment. A good multi-volume encyclopedia for adults costs $300 to $400. The recommended junior encyclopedias, often referred to as family encyclopedias, cost about half as much. They are suitable for youngsters in the elementary grades and will prove interesting to the entire family.

Two JUNIOR ENCYCLOPEDIAS which are widely recommended by librarians are:

Compton's Pictured Encyclopedia (F. E. Compton & Co., 1000 N. Dearborn Street, Chicago 11). 15 vols. $164.50.

The World Book Encyclopedia (Field Enterprises Educational Corp., Merchandise Mart, Chicago 54). 20 vols. $162.30.

Both contain factual articles *arranged alphabetically* as in an adult encyclopedia. They contain accurate material which is well-written for children and generously illustrated with photographs, maps, charts and drawings. Neither set is ever sold in department stores or book stores. They can be bought only through home salesmen.

The Golden Book Encyclopedia (16 vols. of 96 pages each) is much less complete and the price is much lower: clothbound edition (8 vols.), $45; supermarket edition (16 vols.), 49¢ for the first volume, 99¢ for each additional volume or $15.34 altogether. (Librarians point out, however, that the cost per 1000 words is $80 in **The Golden Book Encyclopedia**, $18 in **World Book**.) Articles are arranged alphabetically. They are simply written and illustrated in full color, but many subjects are omitted or covered superficially.

Two CHILDREN'S SUPPLEMENT REFERENCE SETS which are *arranged by topic* instead of alphabetically are:

The Book of Knowledge (20 vols. $149.50).

Our Wonderful World (18 vols. $189.50).

Both are published by Grolier, Inc., 575 Lexington Ave., New York 22, and sold only through Grolier home salesmen. **The Book of Knowledge** is particularly popular with primary grade children. **Our Wonderful World** appeals to older readers.

Both contain nonfactual material—stories, poems, selections from fiction, etc.—in addition to facts. Because they are arranged by topic (not aphabetically), the reader must first consult a general index and then turn to a different volume, perhaps several different volumes. When he does find the answer to his immediate question, he is tempted to keep reading the related articles which follow.

Our Wonderful World is probably the most attractively designed and illustrated reference set for children. The science coverage is particularly good. In some spots **The Book of Knowledge** is out of date in appearance and in content, but it is being rewritten and newly illustrated.

ONE-VOLUME ENCYCLOPEDIAS, published for adults, are more compressed and hence more difficult to read. But two in particular have proved helpful in homes where parents take the lead in using them with advanced readers:

The Lincoln Library of Essential Information (Frontier Press, Lafayette Building, Buffalo 3, N.Y., $28.50). It has 2,000 pages and many illustrations, some in full color. An abundance of information is given under a dozen general headings: Literature, History, Science, etc. A detailed index and many subheads make it easy to find general articles and specific details within the articles and charts. Test questions at the end of each section and extensive reading lists make this a valuable study aid.

Columbia Encyclopedia (Columbia University Press, 2860 Broadway, New York, N.Y., $35 with 1959 supplement). Over 70,000 articles covering a wide variety of information are arranged alphabetically. This volume excludes technical information and has no maps or illustrations.

While these one-volume adult encyclopedias are valuable to parents working with their children, they are no substitute for a standard encyclopedia or reference set written and edited for the entire family.

Why Have an Encyclopedia at Home?

One librarian tells of a mother who asked for advice on buying a children's encyclopedia. "He is only two," the mother explained, "but we want it ready to help him when he goes to school."

The librarian recommended a Mother Goose book for the child's immediate pleasure. "Postpone the encyclopedia," she said, "until you are going to use it." Many parents need such a reference set long before the child can read. They turn to pictures, maps and text to inform themselves on subjects that children are curious about.

Usually a child begins to use an encyclopedia in the third or fourth grade. By the time he is in junior high school he may be able to use an adult encyclopedia.

Many parents buy an encyclopedia to help their children with homework. This is a perfectly good objective. But if the child goes to the encyclopedia only when he has a school assignment, you aren't getting the full return on your investment.

The great value of an encyclopedia at home is in the daily help it can give in answering questions and enlarging the interests of the entire family. The everyday questions that lead naturally to encyclopedia browsing are almost endless: How is glass made? How does a tornado get started? How does television work? What do skunks eat? Who was Guy Fawkes? How does a jet plane operate?

Digging into an encyclopedia for all kinds of information will be exciting for everybody. The satisfaction will be much greater if you have an encyclopedia at home for immediate use while a question is hot.

If you buy an encyclopedia when a child is four, will it be out of date when he reaches the fifth grade and can use it himself? Some entries will be obsolete, of course. That is why most encyclopedia publishers bring out yearbooks, which are annual supplements telling of new developments in science, changes in governments, new faces in world affairs, and so on. Also revisions are being made constantly to keep the content of the encyclopedia up-to-date. Nevertheless, most of the material is little changed from one edition to another. One edition can serve a whole series of children in the family, especially if it is supplemented with encyclopedia yearbooks, current almanacs and up-to-date informational books.

Pointers on Buying an Encyclopedia

An encyclopedia is an expensive tool and a long-term family investment, so it is prudent to investigate carefully before you buy. Don't give in to the fast-talking encyclopedia salesman who says, "You have been especially selected to receive a free set. . . ." or "I can offer you a reduced rate if you sign today." The facts are that encyclopedias are not given away and prices are not cut.

Before you buy an encyclopedia, turn to the school librarian or public librarian for help. Be ready to explain your needs: the ages of your children, the other reference books you have, and what you want to get out of owning a family encyclopedia. Then ask her to show you the reference books she has bought and to tell you the experience of children who use them.

Failure to check carefully may leave you in the plight one of my neighbors describes: "We bought an expensive encyclopedia, but it never has what the children need. Nobody uses it." I looked up a librarians' chart of information on encyclopedias and found my neighbor's set marked "Not recommended." Others in the same price range are classified by librarians as "Excellent" and "Recommended."

Most encyclopedias can be bought only by mail or from a salesman who comes to your house. When you have investigated various sets of books, ask a salesman to call. He will bring a set of books for you to examine and will be prepared to tell you about them.

Insist upon time to look at the books he has brought. If he won't leave a sample volume for you to study overnight, then refuse to sign his purchase order until you can locate a copy of the encyclopedia in your public library or school library. As you browse through the pages, consider such questions as these: Are the pages inviting? Are the pictures sharp and the captions clear? Is the type a good size? (Remember the young reader is used to larger type than an adult requires.) Sample the articles to see how the information is handled. Is the language simple enough to be read and understood by children? How do you like the pictures? Will this material encourage a child to read further—either in this encyclopedia or elsewhere?

One good way to sample a set of books is to look up a topic on which you are well informed. Is it easy to locate? Is it accurate? Is the writing interesting?

Give a thought to the time when your children will be grown. Will this encyclopedia still be useful to you? Sample some of the articles with your own interests in mind.

Encyclopedia prices given in this chapter are the

minimum home sale prices in 1963, cash purchase, with no extra books or premiums. Special bindings cost more. Frequently a salesman will quote a higher price for a "package" which may include better binding, an annual yearbook, and such extras as a dictionary and atlas. And, of course, if you pay in instalments—as many people do —the total is higher than if you pay cash on the line. Except for the **Golden Book Encyclopedia,** none of the encyclopedias described in this chapter is ever sold at discount in department stores or supermarkets.

Getting the Most from Your Encyclopedia

When your new encyclopedia arrives, put it in a convenient place where every member of the family can use it easily. There should be a good light and a comfortable chair near by.

Next, acquaint yourself with the way it is organized. (Remember that in some encyclopedias the articles are arranged alphabetically, and in others they are grouped by topics or themes.)

The World Book Encyclopedia is arranged alphabetically. It has no index, since all articles are in A-to-Z order with cross references (12,000 strong) inserted in the same alphabetical sequence. If your child is interested in dinosaurs, turn to the D volume where you will find four pages of pictures and text under the heading DINOSAUR. At the end of the article, you will find a list of related articles in other volumes: FOSSIL in the F volume, PREHISTORIC ANIMAL in the P volume, REPTILE in the R volume, etc.

Compton's Pictured Encyclopedia is also arranged alphabetically, but each volume has an index which should be used first as a guide. For example, under DINOSAUR in the index of the D volume you will be referred to specific pages in the R volume (REPTILE), the G volume (GEOLOGY) and the F volume (FOSSILS). There is no article on dinosaurs in the D volume, but the index of the D volume tells you where to look.

Our Wonderful World is arranged by theme, not alphabetically. The last volume, No. 18, includes a general index to the whole set of books. Look up DINOSAUR in this index, and it will refer you to Volume 9, which contains a 23-page section entitled "Fossils and Prehistoric Animals." Page references in the index guide you to specific information about dinosaurs in this section. When you look up these details, you are tempted to read the entire section. Many of the articles are from books which are described briefly as well. This is another invitation to further reading.

Once you have learned how your encyclopedia is organized, pick a sample topic and look it up in the index or the A-to-Z arrangement of articles. Then look up the related articles to get a more complete picture. The more you use the books, the better you can guide your child.

In many cases, the encyclopedia will have to be introduced and explained to the child. Help him to use the index if there is one. Explain how to follow cross references. Show him how to find the main points in an encyclopedia article and thus avoid the laborious practice of copying which can only waste time and deaden thinking.

Most important, help him get the encyclopedia habit by leading the way to the books when questions come up.

Each encyclopedia is somewhat different. You and your child will have to become the masters of yours. The odds are that you will both have a wonderful time.

10.

The Power of Poetry

Even a baby likes poetry. He may not understand the words, but he responds to the rhythm. His smile tells you he is pleased.

Later he will chime in on the repeated chorus of a favorite nursery rhyme or simple poem. Almost without realizing it, the child absorbs beautiful language and makes it his own. The vivid word pictures of a poem stir his imagination. He begins to see familiar things in a new light and think about them in a new way. He is expanding and creating because he is becoming attuned to good literature.

A child needs poetry as part of his daily life. When you have read poetry to him time and again, you will find that he comes back to it more readily than to anything else. Not to all poetry, of course, but to those poems which have struck a spark.

When I was a classroom teacher, I found that many children were indifferent to poetry because they had never heard it read aloud. Others had blacklisted it long ago because what they had heard was as awkward and colorless as greeting-card verses. Or they had rebelled against having poetry forced upon them by overzealous adults.

Children learn to love good poetry by hearing it, just as they learn to love good music by hearing it. When they can meet a few poems at a time, without having to

From Favorite Poems Old and New, *selected by Helen Ferris, illustrated by Leonard Weisgard (Doubleday & Co.)*

analyze or memorize them, they respond. I have never known a youngster who did not come around to enjoying poetry.

When my students got on a friendly footing with poetry, they often asked me to read it aloud. Sometimes the children selected their favorites. Often I would choose a poem that fitted the season or a topic we were studying.

Find the Time—Choose the Place

It helps to set the stage for poetry. This is not easy

for the teacher of thirty or more children. At home, with only two or three children, it is much easier.

The time for poetry will vary. You may want to add several poems to your daily read-aloud hour, selecting those that will tie into the other stories or to the events of the day. If your children have learned to love poetry, you could plan an all-poetry hour when everyone can suggest his favorites.

In many families bedtime is a good time for poetry, for listeners are relaxed and interruptions are minimal. Don't overlook the lull on a rainy day or a hot summer afternoon.

When poems become friends, some of them turn up on certain occasions. Countless mothers have quoted the poems of their childhood when walking with their four-year-olds: poems such as "My Shadow" by Robert Louis Stevenson or "Mrs. Peck-Pigeon" by Eleanor Farjeon. A dog down the street may suggest Marchette Chute's little poem, "My Dog," which begins

His nose is short and scrubby;
His ears hang rather low. . . .

If you plan to read several poems, be sure your listeners are comfortable. Children often enjoy poetry most when they can sprawl on the floor. One of my friends always takes a book of poetry on family picnics. She says the bank of a peaceful stream is just right for her flock.

Poetry Is for Listening

Like music, poetry is meant to be heard. This is particularly true for children. Beginners read so slowly that they often lose the rhythm of a poem which they read themselves. Even the nine- or ten-year-old may falter and fumble just when the melody requires words that trip lightly along.

Before you read poetry aloud to children, give yourself some practice. Try reading some of the familiar Mother Goose rhymes aloud and work up from there. For each poem, try to picture and recreate the situation. In "Mistress Mary," for example, remember that you are talking to a young lady, asking her a question. So have your voice make the inquiry with a lift, as though you are speaking to the young gardener next door.

Next, try some less familiar poems, listening to your voice and directing it to rise and fall in a way that is natural and pleasing.

Before reading a new poem to children, read it yourself until you are sure of your voice and of the melody this poem requires.

Selecting Poems to Read Aloud

Success in poetry reading depends largely on choosing the right poems. With very young children you can hardly miss with Mother Goose. (Recommended Mother Goose books are listed in Chapter 1.) For hundreds of years these verses have been loved by children.

I am sure that part of their popularity is due to their singing quality. In fact one of the early editions was called **Mother Goose's Melodies.** Perhaps you know the music of some of the Mother Goose rhymes and can sing "Baa, Baa, Black Sheep" and "Hey Diddle Diddle, the Cat and the Fiddle."

Even nursery rhymes without music have a decided rhythm. Rhyming words and repeated lines add to the musical effect and therefore to children's enjoyment.

In addition, these old rhymes use vivid, exact words

to tell of specific action. Note the first line of three old
favorites:

> Jack and Jill went up the hill . . .
> Little Jack Horner sat in the corner . . .
> Little Bo-Peep has lost her sheep . . .

Each of these nursery rhymes is a miniature drama
with a moment of suspense and a decisive conclusion.
Many others have a surprise ending.

As children grow up, they look for similar elements
in other poems. Although their taste broadens, they continue to appreciate poetry that has decided rhythm, that
uses vivid, exact words, and that tells a simple—sometimes
humorous—story.

Poems That Bring a Laugh

Short, humorous poems follow naturally after Mother
Goose. They are excellent to read aloud to all ages. And
for children who have heard little poetry, humorous
poems make an ideal introduction.

The poems of Laura E. Richards in a little volume
called **Tirra Lirra** are very popular with youngsters of
six to eight or even older. For children who are at the
stage of twisting familiar words into strange combinations,
"Eletelepony" is a winner. It begins:

> Once there was an elephant,
> Who tried to use the telephant—

One of the most popular writers of humorous poems
is Edward Lear. His "The Owl and the Pussy-Cat" and
"The Pobble Who Has No Toes" always delight young

listeners. And his limericks have been read, memorized and imitated by countless rhymsters, young and old.

Unforgettable comic characters appear in many children's poems. "Godfrey Gordon Gustavus Gore," by William Brighty Rands, is the "boy who never would shut a door." Beatrice Curtis Brown writes of Jonathan Bing who "went out in his carriage to visit the King," only to find he had forgotten his hat, and then that he had forgotten his tie, and finally that he was wearing his pajamas.

Another favorite is "The Pirate Don Durk of Dowdee," by Mildred Plew Meigs. This fierce creature was "as wicked as wicked could be" and wore in his belt "a dagger, a dirk and a squizzamaroo."

In "Adventures of Isabel," Ogden Nash tells of a young lady who was about to be devoured by an enormous bear. But:

> She washed her hands and she straightened her
>   hair up
> Then Isabel quietly ate the bear up.

You will find amusing poems of all kinds in two delightful anthologies: **Humorous Poetry for Children,** edited by William Cole, and **A Little Laughter,** compiled by Katherine Love. Both books are good for the whole family.

Seeing Through the Poet's Eyes

Some of the loveliest poems are those that enable us to see the world through the eyes of a poet. Often they show us familiar sights, but the poet helps us find new glints of color and fresh ideas. He gives us a feeling of discovery.

Children respond to the poet who sharpens their senses, who draws them into his thinking and shares their wondering.

As an example, consider Christina Rossetti's famous little poem:

> *Who has seen the wind?*
> *Neither I nor you:*
> *But when the leaves hang trembling,*
> *The wind is passing through.*

> *Who has seen the wind?*
> *Neither you nor I:*
> *But when the trees bow down their heads,*
> *The wind is passing by.*

Or "Firefly" by Elizabeth Maddox Roberts, which begins:

> *A little light is going by*
> *Is going up to see the sky. . . .*

In just six lines, Carl Sandburg's "Fog" leaves an unforgettable image. And in two short stanzas Vachel Lindsay gives a poet's whimsical thought: "The Moon's the North Wind's Cooky."

If you are in the mood for this kind of singing poem, try Sara Teasdale's "The Falling Star" which begins

> *I saw a star slide down the sky . . .*

Or sample the poems of Margaret Wise Brown in that beautifully illustrated book entitled **Nibble Nibble.** Many of these poems are about nature—the stars and the seasons, fireflies and turtles, a rainbow or a raccoon.

A few poets have written about the city or trains and

planes. For example: "A Modern Dragon," by Rowena Bastin Bennett, which begins *A train is a dragon that roars through the dark* and "Cockpit in the Clouds," by Dick Dorrance.

Whatever the setting, the child soon identifies with the poet and finds himself seeing through the poet's eyes.

In reading poetry to children, I have often begun with some of the humorous poems or storytelling poems. Then I have moved gradually to the more personal lyrics. These are the ones I find children asking for again and again. Soon one poem or another appeals so directly to a child that he can say it by heart and thus cherish it for years to come.

Poems for Special Occasions

I think it is no exaggeration to say there is a poem for every occasion. (Remember Christina Rossetti's "Mix a pancake, Stir a pancake . . ."?) Both the poem and the occasion will become more significant when taken together.

If you have been to the seashore, Frances Frost's "Beach Fire" will be especially welcome. Older children will appreciate John Masefield's "Sea-Fever" that begins *I must go down to the seas again, to the lonely sea and the sky.* Even younger children who may not understand it fully will enjoy its wonderful melody.

When you see the first birds of spring, turn to Laura E. Richards' poem "Talents Differ" which begins *What are you doing there, Robin a Bobbin?* and Elinor Chipp's "Wild Geese." If a mouse moves into your house, he is a perfect introduction for Rose Fyleman's "Mice" (*I think mice/Are rather nice*), Elizabeth Coatsworth's "The Mouse" (*I heard a mouse/Bitterly complaining . . .*) and of course, A. A. Milne's "Missing" (*Has anybody seen my mouse?*)

At Halloween, read "The Goblin" by Rose Fyleman which begins *A goblin lives in our house, in our house, in our house.* Or, "Hallowe'en" by Harry Behn.

Christmas offers the opportunity to read some lovely poetry for children. "A Visit from St. Nicholas," by Clement Clarke Moore is read each year by millions of families, I am sure. This poem is available in many editions, some both inexpensive and beautifully illustrated. Martin Luther's "Cradle Hymn," beginning *Away in a manger,* is good to read or to sing. Children will also enjoy "In the Week When Christmas Comes" and "For Christmas Day" by Eleanor Farjeon.

For Hanukkah there are excellent poems, too: "Dreidel Song," by Efraim Rosenzweig, for example, and "For Hanukkah," by H. N. Bialik.

Books of Poetry for Children

You should have several good books of poetry at hand, including at least one well-indexed jumbo anthology with hundreds of poems for many occasions and all ages. Good candidates are **Time for Poetry,** selected by May Hill Arbuthnot; **Favorite Poems Old and New,** selected by Helen Ferris; and **The Golden Treasury of Poetry,** selected by Louis Untermeyer. In most families these are books for adults to use with children. They offer so much that they may be overwhelming for a child to use independently.

Many children feel more comfortable with a less bulky book of poetry—such as **The First Book of Poetry,** selected by Isabel J. Peterson; **I Went to the Animal Fair,** edited by William Cole; and **Silver Pennies,** edited by Blanche Jennings Thompson. Every family should have an anthology of this kind, too.

These anthologies are collections of the work of many poets, of course. When children get to know a particular poet, they enjoy owning a whole book of his poems. Then they can go back to him time and again as to an old friend.

The King asked the Queen, and the Queen asked the Dairymaid: "Could we have some butter for the Royal slice of bread?"

From When We Were Very Young, *by A. A. Milne, illustrated by Ernest H. Shepard (E. P. Dutton & Co.)*

A. A. Milne is such a poet and friend to children. Those under seven love to have his poems read aloud, and a few years later they are likely to read them by themselves. Among their favorites is "The King's Breakfast" which moves from the king's sedate request for butter to his sliding down the banister at the thought of getting it. **When We Were Very Young** and **Now We Are Six** by Milne are delightful books of poetry for children.

Among the many poets who have endeared themselves to children are Dorothy Aldis, Robert Louis Stevenson, Rachel Field, Sara Teasdale, Walter de la Mare, Robert Frost and Harry Behn. Some of their books of poetry as well as anthologies which include the work of many poets are described in the annotated list on pages 263 to 266 of this handbook.

11.

Growing Up with Books

As children read, parents look ahead. They think of the future when their boy or girl will be in high school or college. They wonder about the time when he is on his own, choosing friends and making decisions that will affect his entire life.

Invariably these thoughts lead back to the present. Parents ask themselves: "How can we prepare him for the future? How can we help while he is growing up?"

Usually the questions relate to the child as a person. Will he learn to get along with other people, even those who may be quite different from himself? Will he get satisfaction from daily living? Will he bring pleasure to others and thus broaden his own life?

Intangible goals are hard to measure and hard to achieve. But we know that almost everything in a child's life can influence his growth as a personality. The books he reads are important.

Writers in the 1800's were convinced that through reading a child would grow up to be good or bad. To make sure that each story had the proper effect, they added a moral at the end. Probably no lesson of this kind ever transformed a bad boy into a good one. It seems more likely that young readers skipped these warnings altogether.

Children's stories today do not preach sermons. But many of them tell about someone who has a problem to solve. Quite naturally the young reader ponders the decision that the fictional hero will make. He puts himself in the same circumstances and wonders what he would do. Thus he may begin to develop his own sense of values.

Or he reads of people who are different from himself —of different race or nationality or religion. He may grow to love and appreciate them because he learns to know them. Of course the author's first purpose is to tell a good story. But the child may get more than excitement and suspense from the narrative. All the while he may be developing sympathy and appreciation for the kinds of people he meets through the book.

If so, his reading is helping him grow up as a person who is qualified to live and work with other people. Quite literally he is growing up with books.

Children Have Their Problems

By adult standards the problems of children may seem slight. A ten-year-old girl worries because she is taller than any boy in her class. To her father this is no problem; it is merely an excuse for gentle teasing. But to the youngster this may be the most critical issue of the moment.

Often children hide their deep-seated worries. If encouraged to talk, they may hint of tragedy.

"I wonder why other children do be so mean all the time," wrote one fourth grader. "I have no one to play with."

"My brother has polio. I wonder if he will ever walk again," wrote another.

"I wonder about my father," wrote another child. "I mean, how come he left us."

Many children in these circumstances let their worries and resentments smolder. As a cover-up they will sometimes strike out in a totally different direction with harsh words and even violence.

Grownups need to watch for signs of hurt, such as irritation, shyness and belligerence. These attitudes may be a bid for attention when the child feels neglected by busy parents. Reading aloud for several evenings may restore the warm, personal relationship which the child has been missing.

At this stage it may help to introduce the story of another child who has some anxiety too. The introduction should be made carefully lest the sensitive child be hurt still further. It probably won't help to tell him, "This story is about a boy who is shy too." In no case can we expect a book to cure, but it may encourage the child and set him thinking constructively.

The little girl who thinks she has no one to play with may be comforted and pleased by **Play With Me,** by Marie Hall Ets. The middle child in the family—who suffers because he is neither the oldest nor the baby—may see his problem in a new light after reading . . . **And Now Miguel,** by Joseph Krumgold, or **The Middle Moffat,** by Eleanor Estes.

Children also get a great deal of satisfaction from stories about animals that have overcome handicaps. (For example, **The Blind Colt,** by Glen Rounds, and **Skip,** by Aileen Fisher.)

The older boy with a physical handicap may gain hope and strength from **Johnny Tremain,** by Esther Forbes, which is about a young apprentice whose hand is maimed, or **The Door in the Wall,** by Marguerite de Angeli, the story of a crippled boy.

And the little girl who is bothered by her plain face may get a new slant from **My Mother Is the Most Beautiful Woman in the World,** by Becky Reyher.

Children in a broken home may be comforted by the

very pleasant family life in **Half Magic,** by Edward Eager. In this story the household is made up of four children, their working mother, and a rather unfriendly day worker. The children recognize their responsibilities and cheerfully make the best of the situation.

The timid child may respond to the humor of **A Hero by Mistake,** by Anita Brenner, which tells how a frightened Indian became a brave man in spite of himself.

Learning to Know Other People

Part of growing up is learning to appreciate other people despite their differences. Many storybook characters must learn the first lessons in appreciating other people. When a child reads of them, he may learn too.

Crow Boy, by Taro Yashima, tells of an extremely shy boy in a Japanese school. He is so miserable that he escapes into a world of his own, away from the lessons of the schoolroom and the taunts of the other children. A new teacher takes time to talk to the little boy and finds that he can do one thing well: imitate the voice of a crow. Gradually the other children begin to appreciate the shy one. Their scorn changes to pride in the one they now call "Crow Boy."

The Hundred Dresses, by Eleanor Estes, is an appealing story about school children who at last find common ground with an outcast. The heroine is a little Polish girl who wears the same faded blue dress every day. It is neatly washed and ironed—but always the same dress. Scornful of Wanda's Polish background and her obvious poverty, a number of the other girls begin to tease her openly. Even those who secretly sympathize with Wanda join the tormentors.

This is a story that children like to talk about. Why

The charm did its usual trick, and the baby bounced toward the sky.

From Half Magic, *by Edward Eager, illustrated by N. M. Bodecker (Harcourt, Brace & World)*

did some children follow the ringleader in teasing Wanda? Would it have been different if Wanda had not been Polish? Why do some children like to pick on a newcomer? Questions like these can lead to deep thinking and evaluating.

Blue Willow, by Doris Gates, and **Judy's Journey,** by Lois Lenski, are about children of migratory workers. The migrants move from one crop to another in their old jalopies, always hoping things will be better at the next stop. At each new school Judy is prepared for a rebuff. Janey Larkin of **Blue Willow** wants desperately to live like other children instead of following the crops.

The problems of these young heroines are very realistic ones. Their stories are told with such interest and suspense that children read them eagerly.

Little Vic, also by Doris Gates, is the story of a colt and his devoted stable boy, Pony Rivers. By his loyalty and determination, the boy develops Little Vic into a winning horse. All the while he is opposed and blocked by a trainer who scorns Negroes, and Pony is a Negro. The horse race makes this a dramatic story, and Pony's problem makes it warmly human.

In **The Little League Heroes,** by Curtis Bishop, the boys of the West Austin Little League learn to love the first Negro player on the team and to work together without prejudice.

These children's books—and many more—show appreciation for people who may be different. They are well written and appealing to children. The problems are introduced naturally in situations that are convincing.

When you read these stories, you will see that they absorb even your adult interest. You will want to put your arm around Janey Larkin in **Blue Willow** because her problem becomes your own.

Usually children give the same response.

Establishing Values

Many of the most appealing books for young readers tell of people who are asking questions, making decisions, and taking a stand for what they believe in.

Taking a stand often means making a sacrifice, or a whole series of sacrifices. It may require perseverance in the face of torment, suffering, even danger.

Few children in literature face such odds as Tien Pao in **The House of Sixty Fathers,** by Meindert DeJong. Despite the threats of bombings, starvation and pig-stealers, Tien Pao holds onto his pig and his purpose.

Justin Morgan Had a Horse, by Marguerite Henry, is another story of deep loyalty that wins readers of all ages. Young Joel sees beauty and dignity in a runt of a colt and trains him as a race horse. The devotion between boy and colt, later man and horse, is thrilling to watch.

In some books, much the same kind of loyalty extends through an entire family. **The Cheerful Heart,** by Elizabeth Janet Gray, tells of three generations of a Japanese family rebuilding their mutual home life after wartime interruptions. In several of the stories of World War II, family loyalty helps individuals carry on in the face of bitter hardships. **The Winged Watchman,** by Hilda van Stockum, and **The Silver Sword,** by Ian Serraillier, tell of families in war-torn Europe which learn to improvise and share. The lack of material things seems less significant in these circumstances, and things of the spirit assume greater value.

Twenty and Ten, by Claire Huchet Bishop, is another story of World War II in which grave decisions are made and carried out. Twenty French children living in the country with a Catholic nun agree to share their quarters with ten Jewish children whom the Nazis are seeking. Can the twenty protect the ten? Will even the youngest one resist the candy bars of Nazi soldiers and keep the secret?

The children in **Twenty and Ten** faced a decision that would have unnerved many adults. War made growing up faster—and harder.

The steps from childhood to adulthood are difficult even in a peaceful setting. Perhaps that is why so many children shift back and forth. They hide under the irresponsibility of childhood while seeking the privileges of adulthood. Neither child nor parent nor teacher is satisfied.

Tomi began to rub her mother's slender kimono-clad back.

From The Cheerful Heart, *by Elizabeth Janet Gray, illustrated by Kazue Mizumura (The Viking Press)*

Jody Baxter of **The Yearling,** by Marjorie Kinnan Rawlings, was such a youngster. The fluttermill he built by the stream was Jody's escape to childhood. But Flag, his yearling fawn, was violating Ma Baxter's garden and hence the adult world. Slowly Jody is forced to a painful decision.

Which must come first—loyalty to one's pet or responsibility to society? Youngsters who read **The Yearling**—or hear it read aloud—sympathize with Jody.

Books to Grow On

There's no telling how a child will respond to a book or what he will take out of it for himself. Two children may read the same book on different levels—one absorbing only the adventure and excitement, the other pondering the right and wrong, the justice or injustice he observes.

Some books lend themselves to this sort of pondering —not because the author hammers home a lesson, but because the characters in the story are sensitive people themselves. The reader sympathizes and begins to weigh his own choices and decisions.

In **The Far Frontier,** by William O. Steele, the son of an illiterate backwoodsman is bound out to a wispy little man who roams the woods searching for rare plants and animals. Tobe, the boy, is full of contempt. But gradually he learns to appreciate the naturalist's quest for learning.

"What Then, Raman?" by Shirley L. Arora, tells of a young boy in modern India who is the first person in his poverty-stricken village to learn to read. When an American woman asks, "What then, Raman?", the boy begins to realize that privileges bring responsibilities.

Sometimes the fictional characters grapple with social and economic problems. In **Out of the Mines: The Story of a Pit Boy,** by Frederick Grice, a 12-year-old coal miner shares the misery of the adult workers and the brutality of the mine operator. In **The Knights of King Midas,** by Paul Berna, boys and girls in a French street gang fight municipal authorities who threaten to evict a colony of destitute elderly citizens.

Out of the Mines and **The Knights of King Midas** are foreign books which present realistic, sometimes bitter situations. The American editions are being read eagerly by many boys and girls.

Do American young people see a parallel in some of the social problems in their own communities? Are they developing a sense of social justice as a result? We don't know, of course, and perhaps never will. Certainly some children will think more critically and act more thoughtfully after reading such books. But no book can do it alone. The example of sensitive parents and teachers will count tremendously. We can hope that reading a good book may bring things into better focus while the child is growing up.

Children's books which may open new social vistas are listed with annotations in a valuable bibliography entitled **About 100 Books . . . A Gateway to Intergroup Understanding,** by Ann G. Wolfe (The American Jewish Committee, 165 E. 56 St., New York 22. 25¢).

Five hundred children's books which are considered outstanding for their treatment of human relations subjects are listed in **Books for Friendship** (American Friends Service Committee, 160 N. 15 St., Philadelphia 2, and the Anti-Defamation League of B'nai B'rith, 515 Madison Ave., New York 22. 50¢).

Part II.

How Reading Is Taught Today

~~~~~~

12.

How Reading Is Taught Today

If you stop to analyze the steps you take in reading, it will help you understand your children's reading. For example, when you read the evening paper, you are exercising a complicated battery of skills. You have been reading for so many years that it may seem simple.

Suppose you read the headline:

SPACE MEN REACH MOON

√ *You recognize each word* because you have seen it hundreds of times.

√ *You attach meaning to each word,* but you realize that the four words combined mean much more than the four words taken separately.

√ *You fuse the meanings into an idea* that is still bigger. It is so big it leaves you breathless. What does this headline imply?

√ *You look for implied meanings.* Perhaps your first concern is for the men. Will they survive?

√ *So you begin to react to the idea you have read.* To this new idea you bring ideas from previous experience. You raise questions and perhaps form an opinion. You are thinking as part of reading. As a result you are getting maximum stimulation.

This is a very advanced kind of reading. But it is what your child will have to do before long. His reading lessons in school are intended to help him become a reader who thinks.

An American teacher in Afghanistan saw reading taught with a very different purpose. In one school visitors laughed while the children read very solemnly. "Why do you laugh?" the American asked.

"Because the story is so funny," a native said.

"Then why don't the children laugh too?"

"Oh, they don't understand the story. They are only reading it."

A child in that school is taught to read from left to right. At the end of each line he must turn and read the same line from right to left as proof that he can sound out the words. So he goes from left to right and right to left. In this order the words make no sense, of course. But in that school, understanding is not considered a part of reading. For these children, reading is simply getting sounds from printed symbols.

We expect our children to do much more. Even in elementary school they are being prepared for reading which includes understanding and thinking. That is a great deal more complicated. It is also what makes reading worth-while.

Test yourself with the evening paper or the nearest magazine.

√ *How do you get sound and meaning from printed words?* Some words are so familiar that you know them by sight. They give sound and meaning in a flash. Your name does that for you. So do the little words—*by, for, in, to*, *with*, *from*, *down*—and thousands of longer words, such as *weather*, *baseball*, *hamburger*, etc. You don't have to stop to look at the letters or the syllables of such a word. The whole combination gives meaning as precisely as an arrow on a traffic sign. *You read these words by sight.*

Some words look familiar, but you have to see how they are used to get the correct sound and meaning. For example:

> *Lead* pencil
> *Lead* the parade

Sometimes you meet unfamiliar words which you have to figure out. Often the letters give you the sound. If you have heard the word before, the sound may recall the meaning.

Or you may get sound and meaning by dividing the words into parts or syllables. *Magnetic* means *like a magnet,* while one more syllable gives us *nonmagnetic,* which means just the opposite.

Occasionally you meet a word that sends you to the dictionary for pronunciation and meaning.

There are many different techniques for unlocking words as you read. To become a good reader, a child must be able to use first one and then another.

√ *Now think about the different purposes for which you read.* What you want to accomplish will determine the way you read.

Sometimes you read to get quick information—a number in the telephone book for example. Your object is to read just one line. You do much the same thing with TV programs, timetables and the dictionary.

With a news report or magazine article, you want more information. You don't skim as you do with the telephone directory. But you read quickly if the article is written simply.

If it is a technical journal, you will have to study as you read, perhaps rereading some sections and pondering over others. You will search for implications and recall your own experiences to add meaning.

In all of these cases you are *reading for information*. Each one requires slightly different skills.

But this is not all.

Sometimes you read to learn how to do something—to lay new tile on the kitchen floor, perhaps. Then you are reading to get exact, step-by-step directions. *Reading to do* requires its own distinctive skills.

Suppose you sit down to enjoy a mystery or a best-selling novel. That is something else again. You are just *reading for pleasure*.

Somewhere along the line you had to learn to do this kind of reading too. You learned to let your imagination fill in the background of the story. From little phrases you get a hint of things to come. You are forming judgments about various characters and making predictions about situations. So, although this is fun, you are exercising many different skills.

✓ *Finally, think about when you read best, most easily.*
Probably it will be when you are rested and feeling fit. If you are a constant reader, you are likely to read more quickly and with greater concentration because reading skills improve with practice.

If you enjoy what you read, your interest drives you to read longer and with greater satisfaction. The suspense of a whodunit will keep one person reading half the night while speculation about the World Series will drive another to read 6-point newspaper type in the poorest light.

No machine can measure the force of a person's interest. But in reading, as in other things, most of us give the best performance when we enjoy what we are doing.

Your reading skills have been learned through years of practice. Probably you don't remember when you first acquired them.

These same skills—and many more—have to be acquired by children. How quickly they learn and how well they keep in practice will depend on a host of factors.

Big Charles put a cool leaf on Little Hippo's head . . . .

From The Secret Hiding Place, *written and illustrated by Rainey Bennett (World Publishing Co.)*

There Are Many Methods

A good teacher uses many different methods of teaching reading. She does this so the child will have many ways of getting both sound and sense from printed words.

One way is to recognize certain words by sight.

Another is to figure out the sounds of words.

Another way is to break the word into parts and get sound and meaning from the parts.

Children are also taught to get clues from nearby words.

By fourth and fifth grade, many youngsters learn to use the dictionary, to get both pronunciation and meaning of unfamiliar words.

The Sight Method

Most adults use the sight method in reading familiar words and groups of words. Many children learn to read certain words by sight long before they go to school. An advertiser's name on the TV screen may become as familiar to them as the picture of his product. They read words and picture in just the same way.

One four-year-old of my acquaintance announced he could always read STOP and SLOW on road signs, and on the next automobile trip he proved his reading skill. This is sight reading. Sometimes it is called the look-and-say method.

Most first graders begin with sight reading. There are signs and labels around the room for children to identify by sight. Each child's coat hook is marked with his name —the most important word for him to read at first.

As the teacher talks about the day's plans, she writes

on the chalkboard key sentences which the children dictate:

> *We will read stories.*
> *We will play outside.*
> *We will go to lunch.*
> *We will sing.*

Later the children read these sentences by sight.

Or she may write what the children say about certain jobs:

> *Jack will count the milk money.*
> *Joan and Debbie will clean the cupboard.*

When she reads their words back to them, the children realize that each word says something. Soon they are reading these sentences by sight and enjoying it. But I know of no teacher who stops at this point. Sight reading is generally used as the basis for teaching about the sounds of letters.

The teacher points out that *milk* and *money* begin with the same sound and the same letter. Then the children add more words beginning the same way: *mud, mother, Martie* and others. Later they make lists of familiar words beginning with *ch, sh,* or *th.* Thus, familiar words are used to teach the letters and the sounds they stand for. This is the beginning of phonics.

Two Ways of Teaching Phonics

Phonics comes from the Greek word meaning *sound.* It is a method of teaching reading that is based on the sounds of ordinary spelling. Most adults use phonic skills to figure out the pronunciation of an unfamiliar word.

Sometimes, when you pronounce a word, you realize it is one you have heard before and therefore understand.

To use the phonic method, the child must know when sounds are alike and when they are different. A two-year-old makes a start when he hears the rhyming words of Mother Goose. For example, "Three little kittens have lost their mittens" and "Old King Cole was a merry old soul." He is also hearing words that begin with the same sound: Mistress Mary, Jack and Jill, and Peter, Peter, Pumpkin Eater.

When he begins to repeat nursery rhymes, he has to speak distinctly because the rhymes demand it. Notice this old favorite:

> *To market, to market to buy a fat pig*
> *Home again, home again, jiggety-jig.*
> *To market, to market to buy a fat hog*
> *Home again, home again, jiggety-jog.*

Not even a young child will say *jiggety-jig* on the last line. His ear tells him that *jiggety-jog* goes with *hog*.

Listening sharply and speaking distinctly are good preparation for phonics. Thus when you read nursery rhymes to a young child, you are paving the way to reading lessons as well as giving pleasure to the child.

The steps that begin so informally and almost incidentally at home take shape with more systematic teaching in school. Now children learn how to relate sounds with printed words. They hear a difference between the rhyming words *bake* and *make,* for example. When they see them written on the chalkboard, they realize that the letters *b* and *m* make the difference. This is an early lesson in phonics.

Notice that the teacher begins with words and sentences that are familiar. The child can read them by sight. Now as he finds likenesses and differences in these words, he breaks them down into certain elements. He sees the *ch* in *chair* and *chalk* and learns that these two letters will help him recognize other words that begin the same way.

When he meets a new word—*cheese,* for example—he recognizes *ch* as an old friend. He uses his skill with *ch* to attack the new word.

The lesson moves from the familiar whole word to the general rule of phonics. Because the child can read familiar words by sight, the rule is grasped more easily than if presented cold.

Most schools in the United States teach phonics by beginning with whole words and then going to the letters and groups of letters within a word.

Another method of teaching phonics works the opposite way. It begins with the sounds of letters and groups of letters. The child is drilled on these elements—long and short vowels, consonants, blends, etc.—before he is given whole words or sentences to read. His first reading matter may be a list of unrelated words which illustrate some rule of phonics. Sometimes they are words he has never heard before. At this stage he is not expected to get meaning—he is simply unlocking the sound of each word.

This method has certain drawbacks: (1) The child is learning to piece words together bit by bit, although later he will need to recognize whole words or groups of words at a flash; (2) reading lists of words is so dull that his interest may be permanently dampened; and (3) he is being taught to parrot sounds without getting meaning.

For these reasons most teachers today prefer to begin with whole words and sentences the child knows by sight and use these to show how certain rules of phonics apply.

In **Why Johnny Can't Read,** Rudolf Flesch advocated the system of phonics that begins with letters and groups of letters leading to drill on word lists. This method alone, he said, is enough to teach every child to read quickly and easily.

Why Phonics Is Not Enough

Unfortunately the English language does not always obey the rules of phonics.

Consider the words that end in *-ough* and the way they are pronounced:

> *bough* rhymes with *cow*
> *cough* rhymes with *off*
> *rough* rhymes with *snuff*
> *though* rhymes with *low*
> *through* rhymes with *blue*

There isn't any rule of phonics that will tell a child when to pronounce *-ough* one way or another. He has to learn each one separately.

Or take the words that rhyme with *sneeze* and note how each is spelled:

> *seize, please, cheese, trees, keys, seas,*
> *skis, these, frieze, freeze*

Again there isn't any rule that says how to spell the sound heard in each of these words.

These are only a few of the irregularities in the English language. Phonics will help in pronouncing and spelling many words in English, but not all of them by any means.

When a child faces an unfamiliar word, he should know several methods by which he can recognize it. In certain cases it will help to use the phonic method (identifying sounds and using these to recognize the word). In other cases it might be better to see how the word is built. For example:

1. By observing that the new word is made by joining two familiar words: *highway* = high+way.
2. By noting the familiar ending on a familiar word: *flying* = fly+ing.

Sometimes the child will have to see how the word is used if he is to understand what it means and how it is pronounced. For example:

> *Bow* and arrow.
> *Bow* of a boat.

With skills such as these, a child learns to analyze a variety of words.

Phonic techniques emphasize the identification of sounds. They will not supply meaning unless other methods are used at the same time. Since reading includes understanding as well as pronouncing, it is important that a child learn other methods too.

How Does He Learn to Understand?

Reading is a two-way process. The author and artist present their ideas through printed words and pictures. The reader comes with certain ideas and experiences too. What he gets out of his reading will depend in part on what he brings to the printed page.

If he has some information about a subject, he gets more meaning from what he reads. He can compare the ideas of the author and the artist with his own experience.

This process goes on even as little children look at picture books. When two-year-old Anne first saw Garth Wil-

From The Happy Lion, *by Louis Fatio, illustrated by Roger Duvoisin (McGraw-Hill Book Co.)*

liams' **Baby Farm Animals,** the kitten picture was her favorite. At this page she stopped and stroked the picture. To me the picture of the pigs was more intriguing. But at first Anne had no desire to pat the pig.

What made the difference? Simply that Anne had never seen a pig, but she played with a neighbor's kitten every day. When she saw the drawing, her own experience gave her the sensation of real fur.

√ *Experience adds meaning.* A teacher makes sure that children have experiences which will enable them to get the most from what they read. She may plan a trip to the neighborhood firehouse so the children will be better prepared to enjoy **Hercules,** by Hardie Gramatky.

If they have visited the zoo, they are more likely to get full pleasure out of **The Happy Lion,** by Louise Fatio, and **Elsa, The Story of a Lioness,** by Joy Adamson.

Before city children read about a house with green shutters, the teacher may begin a discussion of the houses we live in. Some of her children have never lived in a one-family dwelling. But as they talk about houses and hear what other children report, they are being prepared for this story.

√ *Pictures give clues to meaning.* The beginning reader has to learn to look for information in pictures. **Blueberries for Sal,** by Robert McCloskey, mentions a mother partridge and her children. "What's a partridge?" a child might wonder. But when he learns to look at the pictures, he finds his answer on the same page. Later his teacher will show him how to get information from maps and diagrams as well as pictures.

√ *Words give clues to meaning.* Often a single word will carry a whole set of meanings. *Houseboat* is a key word in **The Story about Ping,** by Marjorie Flack. To many children it will mean little until an adult explains it. But when the youngster understands that word, the whole story takes on greater meaning.

√ *Combinations of words give clues to meaning.* Frequently an author will use a few words to suggest much more. Poets do this particularly well. "The fog comes on little cat feet," says Carl Sandburg in the poem, "Fog." Your imagination does the rest.

√ *Usually it helps to talk things over.* One of the great

pleasures of reading is talking about it. Through such discussion we relive what we read, sometimes go back to read again, and in many ways gain new ideas.

It is a good way, too, to encourage a young reader to be critical of what he reads. How does the author's experience stack up with the child's? What do other authors say on the same subject? Why do two authors fail to agree?

Such questions—particularly with older children—will help them understand what they are reading and encourage them to think critically. But in every case talking it over should be friendly and informal. Nothing kills interest in reading faster than a cross-examination on what the child has been consuming.

When Should He Begin to Read?

Children do not grow up by a standard timetable. Many begin to read at six or six and a half. Others start on their own long before they enter first grade. Some children mature more slowly and make slower progress. Often those who get off to a slow start gain momentum in third or fourth grade.

Should reading be taught before first grade? I think it depends on the child. Some youngsters in kindergarten have learned to read well. But this does not mean that every five-year-old should be forced to try to read.

There have been experiments, of course, by which two- and three-year-olds have been taught to read. But these have been isolated cases, and the experiments have not continued for a long enough period to show whether the child who begins to read at two has made greater progress at eight than the one who begins at the usual age of six. We know that in some areas of learning—handwriting, for example—the learning process takes less time when it is begun at age eight or nine than when it is begun at age six. Here it saves time to wait.

Certainly there seems to be no evidence that "you should teach your baby to read" despite the glowing arguments that have recently appeared in print. What is gained when a ten-month-old baby recognizes the sign "Toes" placed beside his own kicking ones? Is that reading? And even if it is, will this infant grow up to read any more skillfully and thoughtfully when he is in third or fourth grade? To this last question, there is no answer because experiments have not been continued that long.

One thing we are sure of. A child must acquire a vast array of skills in the first five years of his life. He must learn to walk and run and skip. He must learn to speak the English language, one of the most difficult in use today. He must master the basic elements of arithmetic (size, quantity, volume), science (weather, plant and animal life, hygiene), behavior (honesty, responsibility, co-operation)—to name only a few. When you help him acquire these skills and attitudes, you are helping him prepare for reading in the years to come.

Most children need four or five years to get ready for reading. Yet, even in the first grade, children of the same age prove to be very different. Part of this is due to the kind of experiences they have had at home.

Some have been read to and sung to. They have done a lot of talking and storytelling of their own. Usually they have handled books and know that books are pleasant things to have around. Perhaps these same children have been reading familiar words—*flour* and *sugar* on kitchen containers, for example.

But in the same class there may be children who have done none of these things. Some are from homes where there has been no time for reading aloud. It is not unusual for children to reach first grade without seeing a children's book or hearing a Mother Goose rhyme.

In communities with large foreign-language groups, there are first graders who can speak only a few words of English. In some native American homes children are not encouraged to talk. But children need to be talkers before they can become readers.

There was a day when the first-grade teacher treated all children alike. Despite their differences, she expected all to begin reading the first primer at the same time. Some succeeded and some failed. These early experiences showed that you can't force a child to read before he is ready. All you can do is provide the background that will prepare him to read.

For an excellent discussion of this whole subject, see **Before the Child Reads,** by James L. Hymes, Jr. (Harper & Row).

What Is "Reading Readiness"?

Reading readiness means the time when a child is mature enough to learn to read without undue difficulty. It varies from child to child. Many factors have a part.

1. AGE (The first-grader who is 5 years, 7 months, may need more time to develop than his classmate who is 6 years, 3 months.)
2. SEX (We know that girls tend to mature earlier than boys and, later on, more boys than girls have reading difficulties.)
3. GENERAL INTELLIGENCE
4. PHYSICAL FITNESS
5. ABILITY TO SEE AND HEAR DISTINCTLY
6. ABILITY TO LISTEN INTELLIGENTLY
7. ORAL LANGUAGE (If he has a good vocabulary, speaks distinctly, and can use sentences in conversation, he is close to reading readiness.)

8. SELF-RELIANCE AND ABILITY TO WORK WITH OTHERS
9. EMOTIONAL STABILITY (The child who is tense and nervous or who seeks attention through temper tantrums cannot approach his reading with full efficiency.)
10. DESIRE TO READ

Reading aloud to the child and letting him see and handle attractive books will increase his desire to read. Providing first-hand experiences will add to his stock of information and to the vocabulary he will need to understand what he reads later on. Giving him the opportunity to retell a story or report his own adventures will help him learn to keep the sequence of events in mind. Encouraging him to speak clearly and at length will give him greater facility with words when he meets them in print.

In one city, first graders are given speech training before they turn to reading and books. Children in this area speak with a heavy accent; they drop syllables and slur words. Until they have heard good language, they can hardly be expected to read it. First-grade teachers report that the child who has improved his speech makes better progress when he begins to read.

The Time for ABCs

The time varies with the child. ABC books and ABC blocks start some children thinking about letters at four or five. The television screen makes others letter conscious. By five or six many children want to print their names.

If your child shows interest in the alphabet, by all means identify the letters he asks about. When you show him how to write different letters, be sure to use the same kind of printing (called manuscript writing) that the child will learn at school. (See Chapter 4.)

But don't push him to do something he is not eager to do. Unless he is interested, having to recite the alphabet and print letters may prove discouraging.

A child does not need to know the alphabet to do well in first grade. As he starts to read, he learns to recognize whole words by sight. As he studies various sounds, he becomes aware of letters and the sounds they indicate. Only then is it important for him to identify letters and learn to print them.

Remember Children Are Different

Children are very different—physically, intellectually and emotionally. In no area are these differences more apparent than in reading.

It has been estimated that a typical first-grade group will include children on five different levels—from the nursery-school level through the third-grade level. Only half will actually be on the first-grade level. By the time these children are in third grade, there may be as many as nine reading levels in the class. Children in the same class begin to read at different times and they progress at different speeds. This is perfectly normal.

How Does the Teacher Handle So Many Differences?

One way is to divide the children into three or more groups for reading. In each group children are on about the same level. Those in the advanced group may be reading several grades ahead of the lowest group. Each group uses a different reader. Sometimes several different books are used within one group.

These groups should be considered temporary. A child who outstrips others in his group can then be shifted to a higher group. One who needs to move at a slower pace may be put into a slow group for a while.

Sometimes a teacher will divide the children into temporary groups for special instruction. One might be made up of those needing drill on some rule of phonics. Another might be those who need to speak more distinctly and thus recognize differences in word sounds.

Sometimes temporary reading groups are formed for those pursuing special interests. In one group, space-travel enthusiasts exchange information, tell about available books on the subject, and help each other with technical terms. In another, horse fans compare notes.

When children are divided into small groups for reading, the teacher meets with one group at a time. While she helps one group, the other children have definite work to do—arithmetic lessons assigned in advance, painting or coloring, building things at the workbench.

Another plan, sometimes called the individualized reading plan, is to let each child choose his own book from a tempting assortment that includes library books as well as readers of different levels. The teacher meets with each child individually to hear him read and to note the help he needs with phonics or other skills. Then she brings together the children who need help in the same thing. It is a temporary group that may meet only once or twice for just one purpose. Under this plan a third grader who reads at a sixth- or seventh-grade level can forge ahead, reading books he is prepared for and interested in. The slow reader gets the books and the help he needs.

Some teachers use a combination of the group plan and the individualized plan.

"But that is not all I can do," said the cat.

From The Cat in the Hat, *written and illustrated by* Dr. Seuss (Random House)

There Must Be Many Books

Since a typical class may have children reading on as many as nine levels, there should be reading materials on many levels. A third-grade class may need books for grades one through seven. A fourth-grade group may have even wider needs.

Furthermore, children's interests are different. One boy is absorbed in space travel, another in dogs. If each can read about his favorite subject, he is likely to make greater progress.

When each child reads on a comfortable level, about a subject dear to his heart, reading becomes a pleasure instead of a punishment. But this can only happen when there are many attractive books from which children may choose.

The teacher who tries to teach reading with a single textbook for all children is using ox-cart methods in a jet age. Even if she has three groups and a different reader for each group, but no library books, she is offering pitiful fare to children who are hungry for new ideas. There must be a good library with plenty of books if reading is to be taught effectively. (For suggestions about using your school library and public library, see Chapter 13.)

In addition to library books, every class should have access to such reference materials as dictionaries, an atlas, an almanac and an encyclopedia. Annotated book lists for the children to use will suggest further reading in library books.

Each child should be encouraged to read widely in connection with his lessons as well as for sheer pleasure. If the class is studying early explorers, youngsters can find books, maps and magazine articles to supplement their textbooks. Science lessons suggest an equally attractive array of good books.

When children are free to choose the books they are interested in, they show remarkable skill in finding what they can read and what they want to read.

Measuring a Child's Reading Progress

A child's growth in reading is being checked and rechecked all the time. Two methods are used: (1) the informal day-to-day observations of the teacher, and (2) formal printed tests which are given at intervals through the year.

Many teachers keep a Reading Progress Book with one page allotted to each child. It becomes a diary of his reading progress and the teacher's observations.

Formal printed tests are generally used for two purposes: (1) to measure a child's reading growth in comparison with that of other children, and (2) to find out where the child needs more help.

√ *Standardized tests* are those that have been given to thousands of children all over the country. From the final scores, averages are worked out for each grade. Thus a child's score can be compared to national scores. More important, his new test score can be compared to last year's as a measure of his own progress.

√ *Diagnostic tests* are intended to show where reading skills are strong and where they are weak. For example, the test may reveal that a child can read facts but does not interpret them. This tells the teacher where to help.

A test score means little by itself. Its full value is realized when it is considered along with the teacher's day-to-day observations and the special needs of the child.

Why Promote the Slow Reader?

Often it disturbs parents to find a fourth-grader is reading at a third- or even a second-grade level. Why was he promoted?

For one thing, he may be behind in reading but up to grade level in arithmetic. Why should his arithmetic suffer because he is below level in reading?

If he repeats a grade, he is put with younger children and may feel he is labeled a failure. That feeling does not foster success in reading or anything else. If he has to read the same book again, reading may seem deadly dull.

Most teachers prefer to help a slow reader with his own age group, giving him the extra coaching and the special books he needs. Then he can go ahead with the other subjects in which he is making good progress.

If he is an immature child—shy and retiring—he may feel more at home with a younger group. In that case he might profit from being held back. The situation varies with the child.

If he is having unusual difficulty with reading, the school may recommend special tests to find the cause. Occasionally it may be advisable for him to have the special help that can be given at a reading clinic.

Should the Superior Reader Skip a Grade?

Suppose a child in third grade is reading on a fifth- or sixth-grade level. Shouldn't he be permitted to skip a grade?

Not necessarily. It all depends on the child.

Usually a third-grader is eight years old, smaller and less grown-up than the nine-year-olds in fourth grade.

They might easily overshadow him in physical activities and conclude he is too much of a baby for them. Also, even though he is advanced in reading, he may not be advanced in other subjects such as arithmetic. Or he may be so shy that he doesn't work well with any group. To put such a child with older children merely because he is reading at their level may do more harm than good.

What can be done to help an advanced reader? For one thing, the teacher can give him special help so that he is not marking time while others are reading on the third-grade level. She can also provide him with challenging books that are on his level.

In most cases it is better to keep a child with others of his age. There are exceptions, of course. But holding a child back or putting him ahead with older children may cause great difficulties.

How Parents Can Help

First of all, consult the teacher. She can explain just what is being done at school and how your child is getting along in reading. Most important, she can tell you what you might be doing outside of school to increase his interest in reading and his skill in reading.

At the same time you can help her by telling her more about the child—his interests, his experiences, his comments about school and reading in particular, and the things that seem to trouble him. By comparing notes, you and the teacher may be able to ferret out the cause of difficulties—if there are any—and to suggest constructive steps.

Certainly there are at least three important ways by which parents can wield a good influence on a child's reading.

1. *Read aloud to the child every day.* As he gets older, encourage him to read to you sometimes. Do it in such a way that reading is a pleasure for both of you.

2. *Find books and stories that match his interests.* If he is interested in kittens, find a book about kittens, even though you might prefer dogs.

3. *Surround him with good books.* I am convinced that many children turn to comic books and television because they have no appealing books to read. Don't let a book famine blight your house. (See Part III, "Getting the Books He Needs.")

Further Reading for Parents

Helping Children Read Better, by Paul Witty (Science Research Associates, 57 W. Grand Ave., Chicago 10. 60¢). A 48-page pamphlet explaining how parents and teachers can help children read more easily, more quickly and more accurately.

Helping Your Child Improve His Reading, by Ruth Strang (E. P. Dutton and Co. $4.50). A very detailed guide for parents of both elementary and high school pupils with many direct quotes from children and step-by-step answers to parents' questions.

Individualizing Reading Practices, edited by Alice Miel (Bureau of Publications, Teachers College, Columbia University. $1). Although addressed to teachers, this 94-page paperbound book will be extremely interesting to parents.

Janie Learns to Read, (National Education Association, 1201 16th St., N.W., Washington 6. 50¢). A 40-page pamphlet that introduces parents to the methods and materials used to teach beginning readers.

Sailing Into Reading, based on material by Nila

Banton Smith (National Education Association, 1201 16th St., N.W., Washington 6. 50¢). A 40-page booklet for parents, explaining how reading is taught in the elementary grades.

Part III.

Getting the Books
He Needs

13.

Using the Public Library and the School Library

When children and books come together, reading is likely to begin. For the little ones it may be picture reading. But it is reading. If the books are plentiful and attractive, there is apt to be more reading.

One of your big jobs as a parent is to find the books that appeal to your youngster. Three valuable sources are the public library, the school library and your local bookstore.

The Public Library

Almost every public library has a children's department or children's room. There you will find books to be read for pleasure and for information, book lists, reference books and everything related to a child's reading.

Many libraries are large enough to have a children's librarian—an excellent person for you to consult. Frequently she has printed book lists for free distribution. She also has reference lists with information about many books which the library may not own.

Story hours are popular occasions in most libraries. These are set up for various age levels. Radio, television and films are being used more and more for library programs. For younger children these are usually story-

telling programs. For older children they may be intro-
ductions of new books or book discussions with children
participating.

Find out whether there are such programs in your
community. If so, get your child interested. See that he
has an opportunity to borrow library books introduced
at the story hour or on the air.

A child will feel closer to the library if he begins his
visits early. Take him to the story hour as soon as he is
old enough. See that he meets the librarian and gets a
library card in his own name. Help him find his way
about the children's room so that he knows where the
picture books are and, later, where to find adventure
stories, biographies and informational books. Hasten the
day when he will go often under his own steam to browse
among the books and borrow for home reading.

The School Library

Students who make the best record in college are usually
the ones who were library users in high school. And the
high school youngsters who use their library the most
are those who got the habit in elementary school. No
wonder, then, that most educators agree, "You need a
good library to teach reading today."

Today's children need more books than ever. They
are interested in more things. They are encouraged to
probe deeply and think critically. There is more to learn
today, and there are more beautiful and important books
for children to read.

At school, boys and girls are urged to supplement
their textbooks with biographies and fiction, with tall
tales and legends. Science teachers introduce informational books along with textbooks and classroom discus-

sion. Poems are being read, and folk songs are being sung for added pleasure and appreciation.

Reading lessons go beyond the school readers, and children eagerly seek what they call "storybooks" or "library books."

In almost every classroom there are some library books in addition to the usual textbooks. Sometimes neighboring classes exchange books to extend the read-

The hunter picked up the stick and hit the dog on the head.

From The King's Drum and Other African Stories, *by Harold Courlander, illustrated by Enrico Arno (Harcourt, Brace & World)*

ing of both groups. Or children bring books from home to add to the classroom library.

A growing number of elementary schools have a central school library and librarian. Children may borrow individually, and the teacher may get an assortment for the entire class. The librarian becomes the school's central source of information about books and children's reading interests. She will suggest books and other materials for teachers to recommend to their classes. Often she has a story hour or gives book talks in various classes to introduce appealing books.

Sometimes mothers are enlisted as part-time assistants to the librarian. They arrange and shelve books, charge them out to children or to classrooms, order new books, set up book displays about a special occasion or topic and tell stories. These parents learn a great deal about children's literature and how children react to certain books.

While the school librarian's first job is to advise children and teachers, she knows that parents need help. So she may have a campaign to tell parents about children's books and their place in the school program.

Many librarians arrange a book fair where books are displayed for parents to see and handle. During the day children visit the fair in classroom groups. They are invited to bring their parents after school and in the evening. This gives a splendid opportunity for you to talk about books with the child and find out what he is interested in. Sometimes you can purchase or order books at the fair.

Printed book lists are often distributed by the school librarian. Additional lists of recommended books are likely to be on file in the school library.

When you visit the school, get acquainted with the librarian. She can give you practical suggestions because she knows children and what they like. She also knows what books are available and what they are about.

How You Can Help

Unfortunately many parents and their children have no public library and no school library. The American Library Association reports approximately 25 million people in the United States are without public library service and about 50 million more have inadequate library service.

In our public schools, 10,600,000 students are without central school libraries, and 66 per cent of our public elementary schools do not have libraries. Many elementary school libraries are woefully inadequate. Nationwide, a concerted effort is being made to develop a good library in every elementary school.

When is a school library considered up to standard? The requirements are spelled out in **Standards for School Library Programs,** prepared by the American Association of School Librarians in cooperation with other educational groups. (Order from the American Library Association, 50 E. Huron St., Chicago 11. $2.50.)

Sample recommendations for a good school library:
- At least 10 books per pupil.
- One librarian to every 400 pupils.
- Annual expenditure of $4 to $6 per pupil for books alone.

Teachers agree that the effective teaching of reading depends upon adequate library facilities at all levels. Parent support is needed in the drive to get good libraries for school and community.

School libraries and public libraries are as good as the citizens demand. Because thoughtful parents have been uninformed or silent, most schools and communities have undernourished libraries or none at all. The voters are not accustomed to asking for books. And so our federal, state and local governments provide billions for highways, airports, school buildings, recreation, civil defense and what-have-you—but there is rarely enough money for good library service.

As a parent you can do a great deal to change the picture in your community. One good place to begin is in your mothers' club or PTA group. Women's clubs, church groups, service clubs, veteran groups, and youth group leaders should understand library needs in your community. If you belong to one of these organizations, you might propose the formation of a library committee to work with school and library officials. Learn about school libraries and your public library (or lack of them) and report your findings and recommendations to the membership.

A community library council has been effective in some places. Each member is the official representative of a different club in the community. To learn more about good library services, council members visit school libraries and public libraries in neighboring communities. Local school and library officials and the state library director often meet with the council to report on library needs.

With this kind of advance information, citizens are prepared to campaign for better libraries and the funds to pay for them.

14.

Building a Home Library

In the New York Public Library I once found a Mother Goose book that I had had as a child. It was a large and beautiful edition illustrated by Jessie Willcox Smith. As I sat at the low children's table, I had the gratifying sense of meeting a cherished friend.

I suddenly realized that my mental images of Mistress Mary and Peter, Peter, Pumpkin Eater were those I had absorbed from these illustrations as a child. Here were Jack and Jill, too, just as I had pictured them all these years. It had been so long since I had looked at these drawings that I had forgotten the source of my own visualization. In a very literal sense this book—and particularly these illustrations—had become a part of me.

This vivid experience made me think back to my own copy of this lovely edition of Mother Goose. It had been a present from my godmother, whose Christmas gifts were always exciting. I remembered she had given me **The Water Babies** by Charles Kingsley and Hawthorne's **Wonder Book.** These, too, were exquisitely illustrated.

Those three books I recall in almost uncanny detail. What had she given me on other Christmases? Always something very choice, I am sure, though I cannot remember the gifts. Certainly none survives. Yet even now I have those three beautiful books here in my study.

At Home with Books

Perhaps you have had a similar experience with books of your childhood. If so, I think you will agree there is nothing like having some books that are your own.

If a child owns even a few choice books, he is sure to think of books as friends. They become part of him.

Today books are often crowded out of the home. Space is limited. Families move frequently, and books are heavy to move. Besides, some people argue, there are books in the school library and the public library. Why buy when you can borrow?

Borrowing has many advantages, of course. The most important is that the library can offer a much wider choice than any home. But I don't think borrowing can take the place of owning books.

Certainly I can't recall any borrowed book that has influenced me as have the books I have owned and lived with. Borrowing is for short-term reading. That is just right for some books, but there are others we need to go back to. I think my Mother Goose book meant so much to me because I could turn to it day after day, year after year.

This kind of living with books puts reading on a very personal level. A child who can go back to a book again and again sees it as a part of his life. Even a small home library can build lifelong friendships with books.

When a child has a chance to share in the selection and purchase of the books, his satisfaction may be even greater.

Books for the Home Library

Certain books seem essential to every home library.

Other candidates vary according to the tastes and interests of the family.

Probably the first book in every child's collection will be a Mother Goose book. There are Mother Goose books of all kinds and prices. (See the list in Chapter 1, "Begin When He Is a Baby.") Although there are many inexpensive books of Mother Goose rhymes, I hope you will get at least one that is a thing of beauty. It may seem expensive, but actually it will cost a good deal less than some of the toys and gadgets for young children. Remember: This handsome book is probably the child's first acquaintance with the printed word. Its pictures may be the ones he remembers longest.

Be sure to include several books of poetry. **Poems to Read to the Very Young,** edited by Josette Frank, is a charming collection of forty poems beautifully illustrated for children of two to seven. **The First Book of Poetry,** selected by Isabel J. Peterson, will be appreciated by youngsters in grades three to six. There are also excellent anthologies which are all-inclusive and therefore more suitable for adults to handle and use with children. Several of these are described in Chapter 10, "The Power of Poetry."

Add a collection of famous stories, too—fairy tales and legends, myths, tall tales and well-known animal stories. These stories, like the poems, are wonderful for reading aloud. Many families will add a book of Bible stories, too.

For older children, get a dictionary and perhaps other reference books. (See the suggestions in Chapter 9, "Let's Look It Up!")

In addition there should be picture books, story books and informational books selected for each child's particular interests. Christmas and birthday gifts can add to the collection of books. Enlarge it as each child grows and his interests expand. Then it will be tailored to his own personality.

Enlisting the Child's Help

In developing a home library it is important to have the child's help, so he will have a greater sense of ownership.

As soon as he is old enough, show him where his books are to be kept. Then encourage him to return his books to that shelf because they are his and belong together.

At Wheeling Captain Billy ordered the bowlines ashore.

From Mike Fink, by James Cloyd Bowman, illustrated by Leonard Everett Fisher (Little, Brown & Co.)

As he grows older, ask his help in choosing books. A trip to the bookstore to select a birthday present may introduce him to many books and increase his satisfaction in the final choice.

Some families set aside money to buy at least one

book each month. The choice of the book is the subject of much discussion. In one family of my acquaintance the children frequently decide to buy a book they have all read several times on library loan. Thus, they make sure of an old friend they can turn to again and again.

Bookshelves of His Own

One good way to stimulate a child's pride in books is to provide a book shelf or bookcase for his library. At first it may be one shelf in the family bookcase. Or it may be a small bookrack on top of the bureau in his room.

Ready-made bookcases can be bought in almost any department store or five-and-ten. One of the department stores sells a black wire bookcase with three shelves for $5.69 (28″ tall, 19″ wide, 11″ deep). If you consider such a bookcase, beware of the kind that has V-shaped troughs for shelves. Invariably large books get hooked in the shelf above. Avoid, too, shelves without a back.

Because children's books are often large, there is advantage in building your own bookcase. Even young children can help with the plans and older children can have a part in the actual building and finishing. One simple plan is to pile up bricks for supports and lay boards across for shelving. Then you can adjust the height to suit the books. And when you move, you can easily take the bookcase apart.

For those who are good carpenters, a bookcase with sides, shelves and back is a simple job. Be sure to measure carefully to take care of giant picture books. Better still, provide movable shelves which can be adjusted as the collection changes.

For builders who like a working plan, a scale drawing and directions are given on pages 182 and 183.

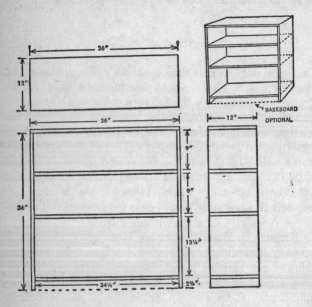

Materials for Bookcase

Top	1 piece	1x12	36″
Shelves	3 pieces	1x12	34½″
Sides	2 pieces	1x12	36″

1½″ brads. Countersink. Fill holes with plastic wood or putty before finishing.

Optional (and recommended)

Backing	¼″ plywood	36″ x 36¾″
Baseboard	1 piece	1 x 3 x 34½″

¾″ brads to fasten backing

For greater strength and stability use 1½" flathead screws instead of nails. Countersink and fill holes with plastic wood or putty. Round off edges of top shelf. Finish with stain, varnish or paint. Use any 1" x 12" lumber—hardwood or softwood. Pine is the least expensive.

15.

Buying Books for Children

When you buy a book for a child, he sees it as something important in your eyes. It may become important to him and nurture his interest in reading. But can you afford the price?

Many of the best books for children cost as much as $2.50 or $3.50. A few cost more. These are hardcover books.

At the other extreme there is a growing number of paperback books, selling for as low as 25¢ and 35¢. Usually the paperback edition has the same text and illustrations as the hardcover edition. For example, **Henry Huggins,** by Beverly Cleary, costs $2.75 in hard cover, 35¢ in paperback. (See "What about the Paperbacks?" on pages 190-91.) Obviously the hardcover edition will hold together better and last longer. But **Henry Huggins** is a quality story in any binding.

In some paperbacks the art work is more appealing and is reproduced more clearly than in the original hardcover edition.

Most of the books recommended in this handbook are available only in hard cover. (When there is also a paperback edition, that is noted.)

If a child reads a book just once, the price seems high. But that isn't the way a child reads a book he likes. He goes back to it again and again. He looks at the pictures and talks about them. He shows his new book to visitors. He may even take it to bed with him. An older child may read a favorite book several times and then lend it to friends.

If two-fifty or three dollars seems like a lot of money for a child's book, consider the cost of these toys, in after-Christmas sales at Woolworth's and Grant's in January, 1963:

Shootin' Shell Smokin' Cap Pistol with 6 shootin' shell cartridges.	$2.59
Xylo-gator, 30″ plastic musical pull toy with winking eyes, wiggles as it is pulled, on its back an 8-note electronically tuned scale.	3.00
Electric Baseball Game.	3.77
Mystery Space Ship, gyro-powered, defies gravity.	3.99
Pot o' Gold, the Make-a-Million Game.	4.17
Battery driven U-control plastic racing car.	4.98
21″ plush monkey with plastic face, hands and feet.	5.88
Kissy Doll "Squeeze her hands together and she puckers up and gives a loud kiss— Lovable as can be!"	10.76
Space Ranger orbiting space station, with vertical take-off, capable of bombing the exploding space saucer and picking up wounded man or messages.	10.97

One month after Christmas or a birthday, take an inventory of the toys and games at your house. Wheels are off trucks. Ladders from the fire engine are scattered under the bed with plastic space men. Strategic pieces are missing from every boxed game. Dolls lie neglected in a corner.

These things represent a sizable investment in dollars, yet most have given only passing pleasure. They haven't influenced the child's thinking or his way of life. They haven't strengthened his chances of becoming a superior citizen.

Children need toys and games, of course. But they also need good books. If you are a budget watcher, remember that the influence of a good book may last long after the little red truck has fallen apart.

Where to Buy Books for Children

If you have a good bookstore in your community or a department store with a well-stocked book section, you are fortunate indeed. You have not only a market place but a splendid source of information.

Pay a visit to a bookstore when you have time to browse, and you will see what I mean. Here are attractive display racks with books exhibited so that the jackets are in full view. Books are grouped by subject or by age level—science, sports, picture books for the very young, etc. Usually the bookseller can recommend an appropriate book for a particular child. Or he can turn to his reference lists for suggestions. Sometimes he has free book lists for parents or inexpensive lists on sale.

All too often parents visit a bookstore without bringing the child for whom a book is being sought. Yet the book displays are very appealing to children. Even a five-year-old will enjoy a bookstore visit that includes a chance to look at some books. This requires clean hands, of course, and due respect for the property of others. But it can be the beginning of real feeling for books and satisfaction in owning good books.

If a child knows that he can help in making a book purchase, the trip to the bookstore will have even greater interest. With his own birthday money to spend for a book of his choice, he feels like a man of the world. His interest in reading and his pride in owning books will increase accordingly.

The better bookstores and department store book sections carry selections from many publishers. If they don't have the book you want, they will order it for you.

The supermarket, the drugstore and the five-and-ten may carry children's books too, especially at Christmas. Usually these have arrived as a package from only two or three publishers, so the assortment is limited. These self-service stores offer their customers no guidance in the choice of books and do not order special books on request.

Suppose you have no bookstore in your town, what can you do? Order by mail. You will get efficient service from the many metropolitan bookstores that have a big mail-order department. Also, some mail-order houses list children's books in their catalogues, particularly at Christmas.

To find the nearest bookseller who stocks a good assortment of children's books and encourages mail-order business, watch for his ads in the major newspapers serving your town. You should also check the listings under "Book Dealers—Retail" in the yellow pages of your telephone directory. Or write to American Booksellers Association, 175 Fifth Ave., New York 10, and ask for the name and address of a nearby place to buy children's books.

Sometimes a children's librarian in the public library or a teacher or school librarian can advise on where to buy books. As another possibility, try your state library agency in the state capital. When you find a satisfactory bookstore or book department, ask to be put on its mailing list for information about children's books.

In some communities a children's book fair is held each year so that parents and their children can see a good array of recommended children's books. The school or the PTA sponsoring the book fair usually arranges to sell books or take orders for books to be delivered later. For further information consult "Recipe for a Book Fair," published by the Children's Book Council, 175 Fifth Ave., New York 10 ($1.25) and "Book Bazaar Manual," published by **Scholastic Teacher,** 50 W. 44 St., New York 36 (50¢).

What You Need to Know to Buy a Book

To buy or order a particular book, you need to know the exact title, the name of the author and preferably the name of the publisher. The customer who wants "that exciting new book about the moon" is the despair of bookstore clerks, for there are many books about the moon.

If the book has no author (as with Mother Goose books), be sure to get the name of the illustrator or the editor.

Some of the old favorites such as **Heidi** have been published in several editions. In fact, **Heidi** appears on the lists of eleven publishers, although sometimes in condensed version. There are always differences in illustrations, binding and paper. To get the edition of **Heidi** you want, know the name of the publisher, which always appears at the bottom of the title page.

If you don't know what book you want, you will need help from your bookseller or from a list of recommended books. And when you are buying for someone else's child, you will have to know something about him. How old is he? What grade is he in? Is he a good reader? What is he interested in?

These are perfectly obvious questions, of course. But booksellers tell me that a surprising number of adults come in to buy a book in almost total ignorance of the child who is to receive it. "I am sure he must be very bright," said one lady, "because his father is very bright." But she was not sure whether he was in the second grade or the sixth grade. Finally she bought a book she remembered enjoying as a child. Whether the young man was as pleased as she was is extremely doubtful.

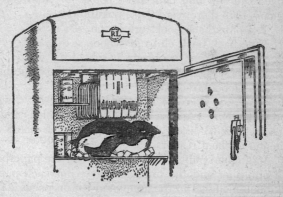

Captain Cook sat most of the day, sulking, in the refrigerator.

From Mr. Popper's Penguins, *by Richard and Florence Atwater, illustrated by Robert Lawson (Little, Brown & Co.)*

What about the Paperbacks?

In recent years many good books for young readers have been brought out in paperback editions and introduced to high school students in their English classes and school libraries. Millions of paperback books are sold annually through high school paperback bookstores and book clubs. Teenage reading has increased proportionately.

By 1963 the paperback trend was rolling into the elementary schools. Close to 350 high-quality children's books were then available in paperback editions. More titles were appearing every month as more and more publishers announced plans to bring out paperback books for elementary school children. The prices (1963) ranged from 25¢ and 35¢ to $1.45.

How can you buy paperback books for children? In February 1963 there were these possibilities:

1. The paperback bookstore at school.
2. Paperback book clubs at school.
3. The paperback book fair at school.
4. The newsdealer in your town and the paperback bookstore or book rack.
5. Scholastic Book Services, 904 Sylvan Ave., Englewood Cliffs, N. J. (Ask for their Readers' Choice catalog, which in 1962-63 listed 200 good paperback books for elementary school readers.)
6. Individual publishers. (The name of the paperback book publisher and the price are given for each paperback book included in the annotated list on pages 205 to 267 of this handbook.)

Buying through Book Clubs

About seven million children in the United States purchase books regularly through children's book clubs. Book club membership has obvious advantages. The child receives new books at regular intervals, and the books are usually of good quality.

Talk to your child about book club membership. If he has a share in making the decision, he will be more interested.

Children's book clubs are of several kinds:

1. *Some distribute hardcover books* selected from the

lists of many publishers. These clubs mail a book to the child at home at regular intervals and bill the parent or other adult donor. Every member within the specified age range—whether boy or girl—receives the same book; he has no choice.

2. *Some book clubs are set up to distribute the hard-cover books of just one publisher.* Except in book selection these book clubs operate like the other hardcover book clubs.

3. *Those distributing paperbound books* operate through school book clubs. Each child receives a list of books from which he makes a choice each period. Books are delivered in bulk to the school, and the child pays when he gets his copy there.

Further information about the various book clubs is given below.

Hardcover Book Clubs
(Distributing books of many publishers.)

CATHOLIC CHILDREN'S BOOK CLUB, 262 E. 4th St., St. Paul 1, Minnesota.

Age levels: Five age groups—

     Picture Book, 6 to 9
     Intermediate, 9 to 12
     Knowledge Builders, 10 up
     Older Girls, 12 to 16
     Older Boys, 12 to 16

Kinds of books: Fiction and nonfiction of general interest, with a few titles of particular interest to Catholics.

When books are sent: Monthly, September through June, or every other month, September through May.

Price: Book a month for 10 months, $22.50 for first two age groups, $24.50 for last three; or 5 books, one every other month, $11.50 and $12.50.

How to join: By mail to club headquarters.

JUNIOR LITERARY GUILD, Garden City, New York.
Age levels: Five age groups—
     Picture Book, 5 to 6
     Easy Reading, 7 to 8
     Intermediate, 9 to 11
     Older Girls, 12 to 16
     Older Boys, 12 to 16
Kinds of books: Fiction and nonfiction selected for interest and variety.
When books are sent: Monthly.
Price: $1.75 per month, minimum 4 months.
How to join: By mail to club headquarters.

PARENTS' MAGAZINE'S BOOK CLUBS FOR CHILDREN, Bergenfield, N. J.
Age levels: Four clubs—
     Read Aloud Book Club, 2 to 6
     Beginning Readers Book Club, 5 to 7
     American Boy Book Club, boys 8 to 12
     Calling All Girls Book Club, girls 8 to 12
Kinds of books: Picture books, fiction, nonfiction.
When books are sent: Monthly.
Price: $1.47, plus postage and handling.
How to join: By mail to club headquarters.

WEEKLY READER CHILDREN'S BOOK CLUB, Education Center, Columbus 16, Ohio.
Age levels: Three age groups—5-7, 7-10, 10-14.
Kinds of books: Fiction and nonfiction on variety of themes.
When books are sent: 5 books per year mailed in December, March, May, September, October, plus a dividend book.
Price: $6 per year when paid in advance.
How to join: By mail to club headquarters.

HARDCOVER BOOK CLUBS
(EACH DISTRIBUTES BOOKS OF ONLY ONE PUBLISHER.)

THE BEGINNING READER'S PROGRAM, Grolier Enterprises, Inc., 575 Lexington Ave., New York 22.
Age levels: Ages 5 to 8 (General reading level: 1st grade plus).

Kinds of books: Beginner Books published by Random House, Inc. (Stories, riddles and informational books about science and nature.)

When books are sent: Monthly.

Price: $1.49 plus mailing charge.

How to join: By mail to club headquarters.

THE FIRST BOOK CLUB FOR BOYS AND GIRLS, Grolier Enterprises, Inc., 575 Lexington Ave., New York 22.

Age levels: Ages 8 to 12 (General reading level: 4th grade).

Kinds of books: First Books published by Franklin Watts, Inc. (Informational books about science, nature, people, places, arts, crafts.)

When books are sent: Monthly.

Price: $1.46, plus mailing charge.

How to join: By mail to club headquarters.

YOUNG READERS OF AMERICA (Division of Book-of-the-Month Club), 345 Hudson Street, New York 14.

Age levels: Ages 9 to 14

Kinds of books: Landmark Books (nonfiction accounts of personalities and events in U. S. and world history) and Allabout Books (nonfiction science and nature) published by Random House, Inc.

When books are sent: Monthly.

Price: $1.85 each, plus postage.

How to join: By mail to club headquarters.

PAPERBACK BOOK CLUBS
(DISTRIBUTING BOOKS OF MANY PUBLISHERS.)

SCHOLASTIC BOOK CLUBS, Dept. RCC, 904 Sylvan Ave., Englewood Cliffs, N. J.

Age levels: Three clubs—
Lucky Book Club, Grades 2-3
Arrow Book Club, Grades 4-6
Teen-Age Book Clubs, Grades 7-9

Kinds of books: Paperback books of fiction, nonfiction, poetry, stories, riddles, with good reproduction of illustrations, some in color. A book club member chooses from a dozen or more books offered each time.

When books are sent:

Lucky Book Club, 4 times during school year; Arrow Book Club, 6; Teen-Age Book Club, 8.

Price: 25¢, 35¢ or 50¢ per book.

How to join: Through a school club.

16.

Book Lists Aid Selection

With so many children's books available, most of us need a guide in buying or borrowing. Fortunately there are many lists of recommended books, compiled by teachers and librarians with wide experience. (My own, "Favorite Books for Boys and Girls," is given in the next chapter. A dozen experts helped to make selections.)

Good lists are available in your school library and in the public library. The larger bookstores have lists, too.

Keep two or three lists in your house for quick answers to book questions and for choosing new titles. As children get older they will enjoy using the lists. Many of these lists are so attractive that they make further reading very tempting.

How to Use a Book List

A book list generally answers two big questions: (1) How can I find a book about a particular subject? (2) What can I recommend for a particular age level?

Suppose a nine-year-old has become interested in Mars and the moon. What books would appeal to him? The index of the book list may refer you to a section on science or on astronomy. If so, turn to that section and you will find descriptions of several recommended books.

Then make a note of the title, author and publisher of the book that looks most promising. This information will enable you to find the book in the library or to order it through a bookstore.

Suppose you have no special subject in mind but simply want a book for a child of a particular age. In the index or table of contents locate the section where books are listed by age level. If there is no breakdown by ages, scan the pages to find titles marked for your child's age group. If no author or editor is given—as with the Mother Goose books—be sure to record the name of the illustrator. This may be the final clue to the book you want.

Recommended Book Lists

Schools and libraries have detailed reference books that tell about thousands of children's books. For home use, a smaller list is more practical.

In many communities lists of recommended children's books are prepared and distributed locally. Sometimes a school will send out a list to every family. In many communities the public library offers book lists on request.

Some newspapers and magazines carry reviews of children's books. Note the titles that sound interesting for your youngster. When you talk to his teacher and the librarian or listen to a television program about children's books, jot down information about promising titles. If you encourage your child to do this too, you may soon have a joint list of your own that will prove helpful on the next visit to the library.

Some of the best-known lists of children's books are described below. All of them give a brief description of each book, the name of the publisher, the price, and the age level for which it is recommended. Usually books are grouped by subject.

Study the following lists and then order one or more for regular use in your home.

Adventuring with Books. (National Council of Teachers of English, 508 S. 6th St., Champaign, Ill. 85¢.) Nearly 500 outstanding books. Revised every two years.

Best Books for Children. (R. R. Bowker Co., 1180 Avenue of the Americas, New York 36. $3.) 3,300 approved books, grouped by grade level and subject, with author and title indexes. Revised annually.

A Bibliography of Books for Children. (Association for Childhood Education International, 3615 Wisconsin Ave., N.W., Washington 16, D.C. $1.50.) About 1,700 books grouped by subject with index. Revised every two years.

Books for Beginning Readers, by Elizabeth Guilfoile. (National Council of Teachers of English, 508 S. 6th St., Champaign, Ill. $1.) Detailed comments about 330 books easy enough for second graders.

Children's Books for $1.25 or Less. (Association for Childhood Education International, 3615 Wisconsin Ave., N.W., Washington 16, D.C. 75¢.) Close to 1,000 inexpensive books, many for as little as 25¢ and 35¢. Revised every two years.

Children's Books Too Good to Miss, compiled by May Hill Arbuthnot and others. (Western Reserve University Press, 2029 Adelbert Rd., Cleveland 6, Ohio. $1.25.) Annotations for 230 choice books for children, with illustrations.

The Children's Bookshelf, prepared by the Child Study Association of America. (Bantam Books, 60¢.) Descriptive listing of over 2,000 books.

Good Books for Children, edited by Mary K. Eakin. Revised edition, 1962. (University of Chicago Press, 5750 Ellis Ave., Chicago 47. Paperbound, $1.95.) 1,306 books, published between 1948 and 1961, are described in detail and evaluated critically. They are arranged alpha-

The hatmaker poked the fire with his stick and said, "Sang Chun, stay with us till spring."

From The Happy Days, by Kim Yong Ik, illustrated by Artur Marokvia (Little, Brown & Co.)

betically by author with a subject and title index that includes a grade-level guide.

Growing Up with Books. (R. R. Bowker Co., 1180 Avenue of the Americas, New York 36. 10¢ in coin with self-addressed stamped envelope for single copy, $3.75 per 100.) A list of 250 favorites in a small illustrated booklet revised annually. Excellent for quantity distribution through the PTA, women's clubs and discussion groups. Also **Growing Up with Science Books.** (Same publisher and price.)

Let's Read Together: Books for Family Enjoyment, selected and annotated by a special committee of the National Congress of Parents and Teachers and the Children's Services Division, American Library Association. (American Library Association, 50 E. Huron St., Chicago 11. $1.50.) More than 500 books are annotated and arranged in 24 subject areas. A splendid guide for parents.

The Science Book List for Children, compiled by Hilary J. Deason. (American Association for the Advancement of Science, 1515 Massachusetts Ave., N. W., Washington 5, D.C. $1.). 1,105 science books for children are classified by the Dewey Decimal System with author and title indexes. A detailed table of contents makes it easy to find books about such specific subjects as Experiment Books, Electricity and Magnetism, Spiders, and many more.

Part IV.

Books and
Magazines for Children

17.

Favorite Books for Boys and Girls

Each year hundreds of new children's books are published in the United States. In 1963 alone there were 2,300. From this vast outpouring, certain titles stand out as those boys and girls enjoy particularly.

Some are popular with almost every child. Others are the special favorites of only a few. The response a child gives to a book will depend upon what he is interested in and how the book is introduced.

On pages 205 to 267, you will find an annotated list of over 500 children's books. It includes many of the old favorites you enjoyed as a child: **Peter Rabbit, Heidi, Little Women** and **The Adventures of Tom Sawyer,** for example. However, the list is made up largely of books published since 1940. They are old enough to have won a place in the hearts of children. When you read them, I think you will see why. In fact, if you are like many parents I know, you will enjoy many of these books almost as much as the children do.

As you look for a book your child will like, think of his interests and his questions. Consider his age, too, but remember that some children are far more grown-up than others of the same age. Some read more easily than others. And almost all like to switch from easy reading to more difficult reading and back again.

So cast your eye on books for more advanced readers and those for younger children. Give the child himself a chance to scan this list. He will see that there are many kinds of books—certainly some that will appeal to him. The books are divided into the following sections:

Nursery Rhymes and Picture Books
Animal Stories

"This is the last straw!"
Miss Pickerell said.
"Just the last straw!"

From Miss Pickerell Goes to Mars, by Ellen MacGregor, illustrated by Paul Galdone (McGraw-Hill Book Co.)

NURSERY RHYMES AND PICTURE BOOKS • 205

Fantasy and Whimsy
Adventures of Children in the United States Today
Stories of Adventure in Other Lands
History in Biography, Fiction and Nonfiction
Fairy Tales, Folk Tales and Legends
Religion, Bible Stories and Christmas
Science, Nature and Other Information
Sports and Hobbies
Poetry for All Ages
Riddles, Rhymes and Nonsense

Within each section the books are grouped by age where possible and arranged alphabetically by title. Author, publisher and the 1962 price are given for each book, as well as a note about the content. When a book is available in paperback as well as in hard cover, both prices are listed. Older books, such as **Heidi** and **Little Women,** are available in several editions put out by various publishers. Although only one edition is given in this list, you will find that other editions are well worth considering.

Happy reading!

•　•　•　•　•　•　•　•　•　•　•　•　•

NURSERY RHYMES AND PICTURE BOOKS

For children 5 and under

Mother Goose, Nursery Tales and Nursery Songs

Book of Nursery and Mother Goose Rhymes, compiled and
　　illustrated by Marguerite de Angeli (Doubleday, $5). A big,
　　beautiful book with many illustrations in soft colors.
A Cat Came Fiddling and Other Rhymes of Childhood, by

Paul Kapp (Harcourt, Brace & World, $3). A gaily illustrated collection of 57 songs, most of them familiar nonsense verses and nursery rhymes.

Favorite Nursery Songs, arranged and compiled by Phyllis Brown Ohanian (Random House, $1). Forty-two favorites with simple piano accompaniment and suggestions for games, dances and finger play.

The Golden Goose Book, edited and illustrated by L. Leslie Brooke. (Frederick Warne & Co., $3). Classic nursery tales (The Three Bears and The Three Little Pigs, for example) with effective illustrations.

The Golden Song Book, selected and arranged by Katherine Taylor Wessells (Golden Press, $1.99). Simple musical arrangements for about 60 familiar childhood songs, including nursery rhymes, lullabies and singing games.

The Little Mother Goose, illustrated by Jessie Wilcox Smith (Dodd, Mead, $2.75). An attractively illustrated collection of the best-known rhymes in a volume that is easy for small children to handle.

Mother Goose, illustrated by Corinne Malvern (Golden Press, $1). Ninety-three Mother Goose favorites with full-color illustrations.

Mother Goose, illustrated by Tasha Tudor (Henry Z. Walck, $3.25). A dainty book of 77 well-known nursery rhymes illustrated in soft pastels.

The New Golden Song Book, compiled by Norman Lloyd. (Golden Press, $2.95). Favorite nursery songs and singing games as well as folk songs, hymns, carols, cradle songs, rounds and a few patriotic songs.

Old Mother Hubbard and Her Dog ($2.25) and **The Old Woman and Her Pig** ($2.50) both illustrated by Paul Galdone (McGraw-Hill). The old nursery tales, beautifully designed and illustrated.

The Real Mother Goose, illustrated by Blanche Fisher Wright (Rand McNally, $2.95). One of the most popular of the large Mother Goose books.

Ring o' Roses, illustrated by L. Leslie Brooke (Frederick Warne, $3). This Mother Goose, published in 1923, remains a favorite, chiefly because of the humorous pictures.

The Tall Book of Mother Goose, illustrated by Feodor Rojankovsky (Harper & Row, $1.95). One hundred of the most popular rhymes with gay pictures in modern style.

The Tall Book of Nursery Tales, illustrated by Feodor Rojankovsky (Harper & Row, $1.95). Twenty-four familiar nursery tales told simply, with delightfully lifelike illustrations.

The Tenggren Mother Goose Book (Little, Brown, $3.95). A rollicking Mother Goose with pictures in full color.

Picture Books

All Falling Down, by Gene Zion (Harper & Row, $2.95). Pictures and text tell of leaves, nuts, flower petals, rain—all falling down. A very reassuring surprise ending.

Ask Mr. Bear, by Marjorie Flack (Macmillan, $2). A little boy who wonders what to give his mother for her birthday gets just the right answer from Mr. Bear. A beautifully illustrated surprise picture book for two- and three-year-olds.

Baby Farm Animals, by Garth Williams (Golden Press, $1). Young farm animals frisk and cavort in charming pictures. Brief text on each of 24 pages.

Blueberries for Sal, by Robert McCloskey (Viking Press, $3). How little Sal and her mother go blueberrying in Maine and meet Little Bear and his mother over the hill.

A Child's Good Night Book, by Margaret Wise Brown (William R. Scott, $3). A charming bedtime picture story of animals getting ready for bed and, finally, children saying their evening prayer for all "small things that have no words."

Cowboy Small, by Lois Lenski (Henry Z. Walck, $2.25). Mr. Small turns cowboy and has many adventures with his horse Cactus. The information is simple but accurate. Also **Papa Small.**

The Duck, by Margaret Wise Brown (Harper & Row, $3.50). Sparkling photographs by Ylla and easy text tell of a duck that goes to the zoo to see and be seen.

Fierce John, by Edward Fenton (Doubleday, $2). A small boy, dressed up as a lion, gets little response from his family until they decide to out-pretend him. Fine illustrations.

A Friend Is Someone Who Likes You, by Joan Walsh Anglund

(Harcourt, Brace & World, $1.75). This tiny book with exquisite illustrations tells how to recognize a friend and how to be one.

Goodnight Moon, by Margaret Wise Brown (Harper & Row, $2.50). A lovely bedtime story of a bunny who says goodnight to everything in his room as it grows darker and darker.

Grandfather and I, by Helen E. Buckley (Lothrop, Lee & Shepard, $2.75). A little boy is delighted by the unhurried ways of his grandfather and protests the rush of everybody else.

Hercules, by Hardie Gramatky (G. P. Putnam's Sons, $3). A horse-drawn fire engine named Hercules comes out of retirement to save a situation that the modern fire truck could not handle.

"Hi, Mister Robin!", by Alvin Tresselt (Lothrop, Lee & Shepard, $2.95). A robin helps a little boy discover signs of spring. Also **Rain Drop Splash; White Snow, Bright Snow** and **Autumn Harvest.**

In the Forest, by Marie Hall Ets (Viking Press, $2). An imaginative story about the animals a little boy meets on his walk through the forest.

Inch by Inch, by Leo Lionni (Ivan Obolensky, $3.50). A strikingly original picture book about a clever worm.

Johnny Crow's Garden, by L. Leslie Brooke (Frederick Warne, $2.50). A quaint picture story of the garden planted and tended by Johnny Crow and visited by all the animals. Only one or two rhyming lines on each page.

Katy and the Big Snow, by Virginia Lee Burton (Houghton Mifflin, $3.25). Katy, a bulldozer with personality, pushes a snow plow during a blizzard.

Little Auto, by Lois Lenski (Henry Z. Walck, $2.25). Simple pictures and text tell about Mr. Small and his auto and explain the parts of an automobile. Also **Little Train** and **Little Airplane.**

The Little House, by Virginia Lee Burton (Houghton Mifflin, $3.25). A little house that was once in the country finds itself surrounded by city houses and traffic.

A Little House of Your Own, by Beatrice Schenk de Regniers (Harcourt, Brace & World, $2.25). A picture book that shows the many places where a child has his own secret house.

Little Toot, by Hardie Gramatky (G. P. Putnam's Sons, $3). The career of a mischievous little tugboat that finally earns the right to be called a hero.

Make Way for Ducklings, by Robert McCloskey (Viking Press, $3.50). The delightful story of a family of mallard ducks that lived in the public gardens of Boston.

Mike Mulligan and His Steam Shovel, by Virginia Lee Burton (Houghton Mifflin, $3). How Mike Mulligan and his steam shovel, Mary Anne, dig their way to a happy ending.

Millions of Cats, by Wanda Gág (Coward-McCann, $2.50). A very old man and woman wanted a cat and got "millions and billions and trillions of cats."

900 Buckets of Paint, by Edna Becker (Abingdon Press, $2.50). An old woman, her two cats, her donkey and her cow set out to find a home that will suit all of them.

Nora Kramer's Story Book for Threes and Fours (Julian Messner, $2.95). Thirty-seven stories by outstanding authors, selected for reading aloud to children four and under.

One Morning in Maine, by Robert McCloskey (Viking Press, $3). Adventures of Sally on the day she lost her first tooth.

Play with Me, by Marie Hall Ets (Viking Press, $2.50). A little girl who wants someone to play with finally learns to win friends. A book with quiet beauty.

The Snowy Day, by Ezra Jack Keats (Viking Press, $3). A small boy's adventures in the snow are told with simple text and exquisite pictures.

The Story about Ping, by Marjorie Flack (Viking Press, $1.75). The adventures of a mischievous Chinese duck that is separated from the other ducks on a river houseboat.

Switch On the Night, by Ray Bradbury (Pantheon Books, $2.50). A little boy discovers that the dark is friendly and comforting, often funny.

The Tale of Peter Rabbit, by Beatrix Potter (Frederick Warne, $1.25). Peter Rabbit's adventures in Mr. McGregor's garden and Beatrix Potter's exquisite drawings have made this little book a favorite of all generations since its publication in 1903.

Tell Me, Mr. Owl, by Doris Van Liew Foster (Lothrop, Lee & Shepard, $2.75). Mr. Owl explains the sights and sounds of

Halloween to Little Boy, who is too small to go out for Trick or Treat.

Theodore Turtle, by Ellen MacGregor (McGraw-Hill, $2.95). A lovable little turtle forgets where he leaves each of his possessions. As he hunts one, he forgets another and thus increases the confusion.

Umbrella, by Taro Yashima (Viking Press, $2.50). Brilliant color and singing text tell of a three-year-old Japanese girl in New York who longs to use her new umbrella.

While Susie Sleeps, by Nina Schneider (William R. Scott, $3). Charming picture story of what goes on while a little girl sleeps.

ABC and Counting Books

A for the Ark, by Roger Duvoisin (Lothrop, Lee & Shepard, $2.95). The Old Testament story of the Flood wherein Noah goes straight through the alphabet to be sure he gets two of every kind of animal. Delightful illustrations.

ABC Bunny, by Wanda Gág (Coward-McCann, $3). Simple ABC book giving a continuing story of a rabbit's adventures.

All Around the Town, by Phyllis McGinley (J. B. Lippincott, $3.50). Gay, lilting verses about city sights and sounds, arranged in A-B-C order.

Ape in a Cape, by Fritz Eichenberg (Harcourt, Brace & World, $2.75). This alphabet book of odd animals has just one illustration and a single rhyming line on each page.

Brown Cow Farm, by Dahlov Ipcar (Doubleday, $2.50). A delightful counting book that begins with one brown horse, then two brown dogs, and so on up to 10. Then each has babies in the spring, bringing the grand total to 100.

Bruno Munari's ABC, by Bruno Munari (World Publishing Co., $3.50). Imagination, humor, bold color and stunning design make this an intriguing book to read and look at again and again.

In a Pumpkin Shell, by Joan Walsh Anglund (Harcourt, Brace & World, $2.95). A Mother Goose ABC book with exquisite illustrations.

Over in the Meadow, by John Langstaff (Harcourt, Brace &

World, $3.25). A picture book with words and music of the old counting song and delightful illustrations by Rojankovsky.

ANIMAL STORIES

For children from 5 to 8

Anatole, by Eve Titus (McGraw-Hill, $2.75). The adventures of a mouse who becomes chief taster for a cheese factory in Paris and earns the title of vice-president. Continued in **Anatole and the Cat** and **Anatole Over Paris.**

Angus and the Cat, by Marjorie Flack (Doubleday, $1.50). A jolly little story of a Scottie pup whose curiosity gets him into trouble. Also **Angus Lost.**

Are You My Mother?, by P. D. Eastman (Random House, $1.95). With only one hundred different words, the author tells an amusing story about a baby bird in search of its mother.

A Bear Called Paddington, by Michael Bond (Houghton Mifflin, $2.50). This little bear with a talent for getting into trouble has endeared himself to children. Continued in **Paddington Helps Out** and **More About Paddington.**

The Biggest Bear, by Lynd Ward (Houghton Mifflin, $3.25). A small boy brings home a bear cub that grows into a great problem.

Billy and Blaze, by Clarence W. Anderson (Macmillan, $2.25). Appealing story of a little boy and his pony. Also **Blaze and the Gypsies** and **Blaze and the Forest Fire.**

Caps for Sale, by Esphyr Slobodkina (William R. Scott, $2.75; paperback, Scholastic, 35¢). After a nap under a tree, a cap peddler discovers his caps are gone, but sees the trees full of chattering monkeys, each wearing a cap.

Casey the Utterly Impossible Horse, by Anita Feagles (William R. Scott, $2.75; paperback, Scholastic, 50¢). The hilarious and thought-provoking story of a talking horse who demanded and expected as much from his pet boy as many children do of their parents.

Chanticleer and the Fox, adapted from **The Canterbury Tales** and illustrated by Barbara Cooney (Thomas Y. Crowell, $3).

"You'd better get me some dark glasses," said Casey, the utterly impossible horse.

From Casey, The Utterly Impossible Horse, *by Anita Feagles, illustrated by Dagmar Wilson (William R. Scott, Inc.)*

The delightful old tale of a proud cock and the wily fox who flattered him, with marvelous pictures in bold colors.

Finders Keepers, by Will and Nicolas (Harcourt, Brace & World, $3.25). Two dogs find a bone and then quarrel over their rights as consumers.

Flip, by Wesley Dennis (Viking Press, $2.25; paperback, Scholastic, 50¢). A lovable colt is afraid to jump the stream, but after dreaming that he flies across, it is easy. Also **Flip and the Cows** and **Flip and the Morning.**

George, by Phyllis Rowand (Little, Brown, $2.75). A highly amusing picture story of a dog that attached himself to a large family.

Harry the Dirty Dog, by Gene Zion (Harper & Row, $2.95). A pet dog gets so dirty that his family rejects him. A bath changes everything.

The Horse Who Lived Upstairs, by Phyllis McGinley (J. B. Lippincott, $3.75). After one try at country living, Joey, a city horse, is delighted to return to his upstairs stable in the city.

Katy No-Pocket, by Emmy Payne (Houghton Mifflin, $3). Katy, the pocketless kangaroo, has trouble finding a way to carry her son Freddy.

Little Bear, by Else Holmelund Minarik (Harper & Row, $1.95). Four delightful stories about Little Bear's trip to the moon, his birthday party, his wishes and his adventures which can be read by many first and second graders. Also **Little Bear's Friend, Little Bear's Visit,** and **Father Bear Comes Home.**

Little Black Puppy, by Charlotte Zolotow (Golden Press, $1). A simple beginning reader about a mischievous puppy who causes problems.

The Little Tiny Rooster, by Will and Nicolas (Harcourt, Brace & World, $3.25). Ignored and rebuffed because he is so little, the tiny rooster manages to become a hero. A colorful picture book to read aloud to young children.

Mittens, by Clare Turlay Newberry (Harper & Row, $2.75). Delightful story and pictures of a kitten who gets lost and is found again.

Mr. T. W. Anthony Woo, by Marie Hall Ets (Viking Press, $2.50). A cat, a dog, and a mouse named Mr. T. W. Anthony Woo live with an old cobbler and have many adventures.

Petunia, by Roger Duvoisin (Alfred A. Knopf, $2.99). The funny story of a goose that found a book and began putting on airs. Also **Petunia Takes a Trip** and **Petunia's Christmas.**

A Pony Called Lightning, by Miriam E. Mason (Macmillan, $2.75). A Western pony is eager to race against the lightning and finally does.

The Secret Hiding Place, by Rainey Bennett (World Publishing Co., $3). Little Hippo, the pet of the herd, is determined to find a secret hiding place and has many amusing adventures in this gay picture story.

The Story of Babar, by Jean de Brunhoff (Random House, $1.95). The entertaining story of a now famous little elephant who visits the city and returns to the jungle to become king of the elephants. Also **The Travels of Babar** and many others.

The Story of Ferdinand, by Munro Leaf (Viking Press, $2.25;

As the soldier whipped out his sword, Alphonse pulled
out his rusty blade.

From Alphonse That Bearded One, *by Natalie Savage
Carlson, illustrated by Nicholas Mordvinoff (Harcourt,
Brace & World)*

paperback, Scholastic, 50¢). A young bull, who prefers sitting and smelling the flowers to bullfighting, suddenly sits on a bumblebee.

The Two Reds, by Will and Nicolas (Harcourt, Brace & World, $3.50). The adventures of a boy and a cat in a big city. Brilliant pictures.

For children from 9 to 12

Afraid to Ride, by C. W. Anderson (Macmillan, $3; paperback, Scholastic, 35¢). How Judy overcame her fears after a bad fall from a horse that had been mistreated.

Along Came a Dog, by Meindert DeJong (Harper & Row, $2.95). A dramatic story of a homeless dog, a little red hen and a man who talked to animals.

Alphonse That Bearded One, by Natalie Savage Carlson (Harcourt, Brace & World, $2.95). Canadian folk tale of a bear cub, trained to be a soldier, who takes his master's place in the army.

The Blind Colt, by Glen Rounds (Holiday House, $2.95). A colt, born blind, grows up with a mustang band and then is adopted and trained by a ten-year-old boy in South Dakota.

Blue Canyon Horse, by Ann Nolan Clark (Viking Press, $2.75). A poetic story of a little mare who deserts an Indian boy to enjoy the freedom of the wild.

Brighty of the Grand Canyon, by Marguerite Henry (Rand McNally, $3.50). An old prospector finds a little wild burro on Bright Angel Creek in the Grand Canyon, and a lasting friendship develops.

Cat Tales, by Natalia M. Belting (Holt, Rinehart & Winston, $3). Sixteen cat tales from various parts of the world, retold with flavor.

Duff, the Story of a Bear, by William Marshall Rush (David McKay, $3). The exciting life story of a black bear in the Rockies.

Elsa, the Story of a Lioness, by Joy Adamson (Pantheon Books, $3.50). A beautiful photo story of the lioness who was brought up by the author and then taught to stalk and kill for herself in the African jungle.

Friends to Man, the Wonderful World of Animals, compiled by Frances Cavanah (Macrae Smith, $3.50). Twenty-six animal stories, both fact and fiction, by outstanding authors.

The Golden Mare, by William Corbin (Coward-McCann, $3). An exciting horse story for better readers.

Grishka and the Bear, by René Guillot (Criterion Books, $2.75). An enthralling tale of a boy in northern Siberia whose young cub is feted by the tribesmen until the time comes when he must be sacrificed at the festival of the bear.

Honk the Moose, by Phil Stong (Dodd, Mead, $3). Two boys discover a moose in their stable and figure out a solution to the strange problem.

Justin Morgan Had a Horse, by Marguerite Henry (Rand McNally, $3.50). Story of the brave little Vermont work horse from which came the long line of Morgan horses.

Kildee House, by Rutherford Montgomery (Doubleday, $2.95). When Jerome Kildee retires to live in a mountain cabin, he has fun and problems galore with the raccoons and skunks that come to live with him.

King of the Wind, by Marguerite Henry (Rand McNally, $3.50). A spirited Arabian horse and a mute stableboy become fast friends.

Lassie Come-Home, by Eric Knight (Holt, Rinehart & Winston, $2.95; paperback, Grosset & Dunlap, 50¢). A collie dog, taken hundreds of miles from home, makes her way back to meet her master at the schoolhouse gate.

Little Vic, by Doris Gates (Viking Press, $2.50). A Negro stableboy helps Little Vic win the Santa Anita Handicap and at the same time breaks down the prejudice of his white trainer.

Misty of Chincoteague, by Marguerite Henry (Rand McNally, $3.50). At the spring roundup of wild ponies from Chincoteague Island, two children adopt a wild pony. Continued in **Sea Star.**

Mountain Born, by Elizabeth Yates (Coward-McCann, $3.50). The beautifully written story of a boy and his black lamb. Continued in **A Place for Peter.**

Old Bones, the Wonder Horse, by Mildred Mastin Pace (Mc-

Graw-Hill, $3.25; paperback, Scholastic, 50¢). The rags-to-riches story of a horse that came out of nowhere to win the Kentucky Derby.

Plug-Horse Derby, by Emma L. Brock (Alfred A. Knopf, $2.75). A little girl trains her entry for a plow horse derby and wins.

Ringtail, by Alice Crew Gall and Fleming H. Crew (Henry Z. Walck, $3). The adventures of a young raccoon from early spring to snowfall.

Skip, by Aileen Fisher (Thomas Nelson, $2.95; paperback, Scholastic, 35¢). How a little girl helps her blind dog earn his right to survival on the farm.

Taffy's Foal, by Elisa Bialk (Houghton Mifflin, $3). Nancy accepts her new stepmother and the move to the city, but she cannot leave her horse.

For better readers of 12 and up

Big Red, by Jim Kjelgaard (Holiday House, $2.95; paperback, Scholastic, 50¢). The adventures of an Irish setter and Danny, his trainer, and their triumph over a great bear in the Wintapi wilderness.

The Black Stallion, by Walter Farley (Random House, $2.50). There's breathtaking excitement in this story of a boy, a wild black stallion, a shipwreck and a horse race. Also **Son of the Black Stallion, The Black Stallion and Satan,** and **The Island Stallion.**

Dipper of Copper Creek, by John L. George and Jean George (E. P. Dutton, $3.50). A beautifully detailed story of wildlife in the Colorado Rockies, where an old miner and his grandson save a fledgling water ouzel.

Gunilla, an Arctic Adventure, by Alfred Viksten (Thomas Nelson, $2.75). The first-person story of a lone hunter on Spitsbergen, who adopts a polar bear cub and later must battle her for his life.

The Incredible Journey, a Tale of Three Animals, by Sheila Burnford (Little, Brown, $3.75; paperback, Bantam, 50¢). A Siamese cat, an English bull terrier and a Labrador retriever make their way painfully over hundreds of miles to get home again.

Vulpes, the Red Fox, by John L. George and Jean George (E. P. Dutton, $3.50). The life story of a red fox born and reared in the Maryland hills.

FANTASY AND WHIMSY

For children from 5 to 8

The Adventures of Pinocchio, by Collodi (Macmillan, $2.75). This story of a saucy little puppet whose nose grows longer every time he tells a lie is as popular today as when it first appeared in Italy many years ago.

And to Think That I Saw It on Mulberry Street, by Dr. Seuss (Vanguard Press, $2.95). A horse-drawn wagon on Mulberry Street grows bigger and bigger as a small boy plans how he will tell about it when he gets home. The illustrations show his vision growing to fantastic proportions.

Andy and the Lion, by James Daugherty (Viking Press, $3). An amusing version of the old story of the boy who pulled a thorn out of the lion's paw and thereby made a friend.

The Camel Who Took a Walk, by Jack Tworkov (E. P. Dutton, $2.75). Humorous suspense story of a camel, a tiger, a monkey, a squirrel and a bird.

The Cat in the Hat, by Dr. Seuss (Random House, $1.95). Hilarious story in verse of the wacky performance of a cat that comes to visit on a rainy day. Can be read by many first graders. Also, **The Cat in the Hat Comes Back.**

Crictor, by Tomi Ungerer (Harper & Row, $2.95). The hilarious picture story of a boa constrictor which is the pet of an elderly French schoolmistress.

Curious George, by H. A. Rey (Houghton Mifflin, $3.25). After wild adventures in a big city, George, a monkey with great curiosity, finds himself in a nice safe zoo. Continued in **Curious George Takes a Job, Curious George Rides a Bike** and others.

Danny and the Dinosaur, by Syd Hoff (Harper & Row, $1.95). There is lovely spoofing in this easy-to-read book about a boy and a museum dinosaur on the town for a day.

The Duchess Bakes a Cake, by Virginia Kahl (Charles Scribner's Sons, $3.25). The comical story of the Duchess who added yeast to her cake "six times for good measure" and was carried into the sky as it rose. Her rescue is the great surprise.

The Fast Sooner Hound, by Arna Bontemps and Jack Conroy (Houghton Mifflin, $3.75). A tall tale of a flop-eared hound that beat the local, the freight and the express.

The Five Chinese Brothers, by Claire Huchet Bishop (Coward-McCann, $2.50; paperback, Scholastic, 50¢). An old Chinese tale retold with exaggerated humor.

The 500 Hats of Bartholomew Cubbins, by Dr. Seuss (Vanguard Press, $2.95). Hilarious story of a boy who takes off his hat before the King but finds another in its place, then another and another.

Georgie, by Robert Bright (Doubleday, $2). Every evening a gentle little ghost named Georgie disturbs the family by stepping on a loose board and swinging a squeaky door. Also **Georgie to the Rescue.**

The Happy Lion, by Louise Fatio (McGraw-Hill, $2.75). When the happy lion escapes from the zoo in a French town, he is dismayed to find people running away from him. Also **The Happy Lion Roars, The Happy Lion in Africa,** and **The Three Happy Lions.**

Horton Hatches the Egg, by Dr. Seuss (Random House, $2.95). Horton, the faithful elephant, finds himself sitting on the nest of Mayzie the lazy bird, hatching her egg. A comical situation told in verse with bold illustrations.

Little Tim and the Brave Sea Captain, by Edward Ardizzone (Henry Z. Walck, $3). A vivid story of life at sea with a five-year-old boy as hero. Continued in **Tim to the Rescue** and others.

Miss Flora McFlimsey's Easter Bonnet, by Mariana (Lothrop, Lee & Shepard, $1.50). How an old neglected doll gets a new Easter bonnet, the gift from the rabbit Peterkin.

The Most Wonderful Doll in the World, by Phyllis McGinley (J. B. Lippincott, $2.95). The adventures of a doll that lived only in the imagination of a little girl.

My Father's Dragon, by Ruth Stiles Gannett (Random House, $2.95). How a little boy rescues a baby dragon by appealing to the greed and conceit of the fierce creatures on Wild Island.

Winnie-the-Pooh, by A. A. Milne (E. P. Dutton, $2.95). A favorite read-aloud book about six-year-old Christopher Robin and his toy pets, especially Winnie-the-Pooh, the adored Teddy bear. Continued in **The House at Pooh Corner.**

For children from 9 to 12

Alice's Adventures in Wonderland and **Through the Looking Glass,** by Lewis Carroll with original Tenniel illustrations (Macmillan, $3; paperback, New American Library, 50¢). The classic story of the little girl who followed a rabbit down its hole into a land of enchantment and magical events.

The Blue Cat of Castle Town, by Catherine Cate Coblentz (David McKay Co., $3.50). A blue kitten learns the song of the river near his small Vermont town and brings its magic to his owner.

The Blue-Nosed Witch, by Margaret Embry (Holiday House, $2.25). Blanche, a modern young witch with a nose she can make glow in the dark, joins Halloweeners on a trick-or-treat expedition.

The Borrowers, by Mary Norton (Harcourt, Brace & World, $2.95). About the inhabitants of a fascinating miniature world who live by borrowing what they need. Also **The Borrowers Afield, The Borrowers Afloat** and **The Borrowers Aloft.**

Charlotte's Web, by E. B. White (Harper & Row, $2.95). Charlotte, a thoughtful spider, who saves the life of a doomed pig by spinning messages in her web, has become the most loved spider of all time.

The Children of Green Knowe, by L. M. Boston (Harcourt, Brace & World, $2.75). A delightful read-aloud fantasy about a little English boy who comes to live with his great-grandmother and succeeds in winning the friendship of three seventeenth century children whose portrait is over the fireplace. Also, **Treasure of Green Knowe.**

The Cricket in Times Square, by George Selden (Farrar, Straus and Co., $3.50). The wonderful story of a cricket from Connecticut who spends the summer in a New York subway sta-

Tucker Mouse scrambled into the cage and looked around. "I feel like the Emperor of China," he said.

From The Cricket of Times Square, *by George Selden, illustrated by Garth Williams (Farrar, Straus & Co.)*

tion, aided and abetted by three friends—a boy, a cat and a fast-talking Broadway mouse.

Danny Dunn and the Anti-Gravity Paint, by Jay Williams and Raymond Abrashkin (McGraw-Hill, $2.95; paperback, Scholastic, 35¢). A convincing tale of the flight of Danny and his pal in a space ship between planets—all made possible by Danny's chance discovery of anti-gravity paint. Continued in **Danny Dunn and the Homework Machine, Danny Dunn and the Weather Machine** and others.

The Enormous Egg, by Oliver Butterworth (Little, Brown, $2.95; paperback, Scholastic, 50¢). A twelve-year-boy has an enormous egg which finally hatches a dinosaur.

Freddy the Detective, by Walter R. Brooks (Alfred A. Knopf, $3; paperback, Scholastic, 50¢). Fantastic story of Freddy the pig and his amazing escapades. Also **Freddy the Cowboy, Freddy Goes to Mars, Freddy and the Space Ship,** and many more.

Ghosts and Goblins, edited by Wilhelmina Harper (E. P. Dutton, $3.50). A fine collection of stories and poems about Halloween.

Half Magic, by Edward Eager (Harcourt, Brace & World, $2.95). As a result of the half magic created by a strange old coin, Jane, her two sisters, and her brother have unequaled adventures in time and space. Also **Magic or Not?**

The Lion, the Witch and the Wardrobe, by C. S. Lewis (Macmillan, $3). Four children, in the country to escape London air raids during World War II, have exciting adventures in the mysterious land of Narnia, just beyond the wardrobe in a vacant room. Continued in **The Magician's Nephew, The Last Battle,** and others.

Little Witch, by Anna Elizabeth Bennett (J. B. Lippincott & Co., $2.95; paperback, Scholastic, 50¢). Humor and fantasy are combined in this story of the little witch who rides to school on a broomstick.

The Magic Chalk, by Zinken Hopp (David McKay, $2.75). John finds a piece of magic chalk with which he draws a pal who comes to life. Together they draw their way in and out of fabulous adventures.

Many Moons, by James Thurber (Harcourt, Brace & World,

$3.50). Fantasy of the little princess who wanted the moon—and got it.

Mary Poppins, by Pamela Travers (Harcourt, Brace & World, $3.25). Charming nonsense about a nursemaid who blew in with the east wind and slid gracefully up the banister.

Miss Pickerell Goes to Mars, by Ellen MacGregor (McGraw-Hill, $2.50; paperback, Scholastic, 50¢). Precise Miss Pickerell, who wouldn't venture on a Ferris wheel, suddenly finds herself whisked off to another planet. Also **Miss Pickerell Goes to the Arctic, Miss Pickerell Goes Underseas,** and **Miss Pickerell and the Geiger Counter.**

Mr. Popper's Penguins, by Richard and Florence Atwater (Little, Brown, $3.50). Mr. Popper turns over his house to Captain Cook, a penguin presented by an Antarctic explorer. Before long twelve penguins are ruling the Popper household.

The Mountain Door, by Rosalie Fry (E. P. Dutton, $2.95). A delicate story of two little girls who meet at the door of a fairy-haunted mountain in Ireland and wander the countryside with a dog, a donkey, a cow and some ducks.

Padre Porko, the Gentlemanly Pig, by Robert Davis (Holiday House, $3). Folk tales of the genial pig who speaks any language and devotes his ingenuity to helping all creatures—animal and human alike.

The Peterkin Papers, by Lucretia P. Hale (Dover, paperbound, $1). These stories of a completely scatterbrained family are ideal for reading aloud.

Pippi Longstocking, by Astrid Lindgren (Viking Press, $2; paperback, Scholastic, 35¢). Nine-year-old Pippi lives alone except for her monkey, her horse and her fortune in gold pieces, but she manages to create a sensation wherever she goes. Her adventures continue in **Pippi Goes on Board** and **Pippi in the South Seas.**

Rabbit Hill, by Robert Lawson (Viking Press, $3). When new folks come to the big house, the animals on Rabbit Hill have many interesting adventures. Continued in **The Tough Winter.**

The Reluctant Dragon, by Kenneth Grahame (Holiday House, $2.50). Amusing story of the boy who made friends with a peace-loving dragon.

The Rescuers, by Margery Sharp (Little, Brown, $3.75). This delightful fantasy about three mice which undertake to rescue a Norwegian poet imprisoned in the grim, windowless Black Castle is fine to read aloud.

The Shy Stegosaurus of Cricket Creek, by Evelyn Sibley Lampman (Doubleday, $2.95; paperback, Scholastic, 50¢). While they are hunting fossils on Cricket Creek, the Brown twins meet George, a shy stegosaurus.

Space Cat, by Ruthven Todd (Charles Scribner's Sons, $2.75). The adventures of Flyball, the cat that goes by rocket ship to outer space. Also, **Space Cat Visits Venus** and **Space Cat Meets Mars.**

The Twenty-One Balloons, by William Pène du Bois (Viking Press, $3). Fantasy, science and adventure are in this story of Professor William Waterman Sherman, who starts out in one balloon and is picked up in the Atlantic in the wreckage of twenty balloons.

When the Mississippi Was Wild, by LeGrand (Abingdon Press, $2). Tall tale of Mike Fink, champion fighter, who battled Old Al, the alligator, and tied his tail halfway so he could raise nothing more than a half-tail storm on the river. Also **Cap'n Dow and the Hole in the Doughnut** and **Why Cowboys Sing, in Texas.**

The Wind in the Willows, by Kenneth Grahame (Charles Scribner's Sons, $2.95 hardcover; $1.45 paperback). The classic story of Mole, Water Rat, Badger and Toad and their life in the woods and along the banks of the Thames.

The Wizard of Oz and **The Land of Oz,** by L. Frank Baum (Looking Glass Library, $1.95; paperback, Scholastic, 50¢; paperback, Fawcett, 35¢). Popular fantasy about the Wizard, the Scarecrow, the Tin Woodman and the Diamond-Studded Dishpan.

The Wonderful Flight to the Mushroom Planet, by Eleanor Cameron (Little, Brown, $3). Two boys build a space ship and journey to a distant planet.

ADVENTURES OF CHILDREN IN THE
UNITED STATES TODAY

For children from 5 to 8

"B" Is for Betsy, by Carolyn Haywood (Harcourt, Brace & World, $3.50). The first year of school for a typical American girl. Also **Back to School with Betsy, Betsy and Billy, Betsy and the Boys.**

Beanie, by Ruth and Latrobe Carroll (Henry Z. Walck, $2.75). The adventures of a small boy and his puppy, Tough Enough, in the Great Smoky Mountains. Continued in **Tough Enough, Tough Enough's Trip,** and **Tough Enough's Pony.**

Come to the Zoo, by Ruth M. Tensen (Reilly & Lee, $2.75). Sharp photographs and simple text tell of a trip to the zoo. Second-grade reading level. Also **Come to the Farm.**

Cowboy Sam, by Edna Walker Chandler (Benefic Press, $1.60). First in a series of eight stories about cattle roundups, rattle-snakes, wolves and all the events of ranch life. Can be read by many first-graders.

Down, Down the Mountain, by Ellis Credle (Thomas Nelson Sons, $2). Two children of the Blue Ridge Mountains raise turnips which they hope to trade for squeaky shoes.

I Know a Farm, by Ethel Collier (William R. Scott, $3). With a vocabulary of only 177 words, this story can be read by beginners who will enjoy a child's solitary exploration of a farmer's barn.

In My Mother's House, by Ann Nolan Clark (Viking Press, $3). An exquisite story of the daily life of an Indian child in the Southwest, written in rhythmic prose.

Indian Two Feet and His Horse, by Margaret Friskey (Childrens Press, $2.50). An Indian boy, told to use his own two feet, goes out and finds himself a horse. An easy book for the beginner.

Lentil, by Robert McCloskey (Viking Press, $3.50). Practice in the bathtub improves Lentil's harmonica-playing to the point where he wins real distinction.

Little Eddie, by Carolyn Haywood (William Morrow, $3.50). The adventures of a seven-year-old who knows what he wants and goes after it. Also **Eddie's Pay Dirt, Eddie and Gardenia, Eddie and His Big Deals.**

Lucy McLockett, by Phyllis McGinley (J. B. Lippincott, $3.50). A charming verse and prose story of a little girl who loses everything. Good for reading aloud to children of seven and under.

Moy Moy, by Leo Politi (Charles Scribner's Sons, $2.95). The story of a Chinese-American girl living on Chanking Street in Los Angeles where the Chinese New Year is celebrated with a dragon parade. Also **Juanita,** the story of a Mexican-American girl in Los Angeles.

Nobody Listens to Andrew, by Elizabeth Guilfoile (Follett, $1). The simple story of a boy with big news which is ignored by all until the final big surprise. For beginning readers.

Roger and the Fox, by Lavinia Davis (Doubleday, $2.75). Roger's search for the fox, his fun on skis, and the snow-clad Connecticut countryside combine to make this book too good to miss.

Song of the Swallows, by Leo Politi (Charles Scribner's Sons, $3.25). The friendship between a little boy and the old gardener who was bell ringer at the Mission of San Juan Capistrano in California.

Two Is a Team, by Lorraine and Jerrold Beim (Harcourt, Brace & World, $2.75). As a little Negro boy and a little white boy learn to co-operate, they gain genuine satisfaction.

We Live in the South, by Lois Lenski (J. B. Lippincott, $3.50). Three simple stories with realistic details about life in the Southeastern pine woods, in the Negro quarter of a Southern town, and in a Florida orange grove. Also, **We Live in the City, We Live in the Country,** and **We Live in the Southwest.**

Whitey and the Colt-Killer, by Glen Rounds (Holiday House, $2.50). Whitey and Josie, pint-sized cowhands, fight a prairie fire and trail a wily colt-killing wolf. Also, **Whitey's First Roundup, Whitey Ropes and Rides** and several more.

For children from 9 to 12

Ballet for Mary, by Emma L. Brock (Alfred A. Knopf, $2.75). An amusing story of Sudden Mary (so named because she always moves in sudden jerks) and her efforts to become a ballerina.

The Beatinest Boy, by Jesse Stuart (McGraw-Hill, $2.50). Orphaned David is brought up in the Kentucky mountains by his grandmother who teaches him to hunt, to cut a bee tree and to save the puppy named Orphan. A tender relationship between boy and grandmother.

Blue Willow, by Doris Gates (Viking Press, $3; paperback, Scholastic, 50¢). For five years ten-year-old Janey Larkin and her family follow the crops as migratory workers.

Bright April, by Marguerite de Angeli (Doubleday, $2.75). The heart-warming story of a ten-year-old Negro girl who is active in a Brownie troop in Philadelphia.

Then into the fray came a cannonball of fur and teeth.

From A Dog on Barkham Street, *by M. S. Stoltz, illustrated by Leonard Shortall (Harper & Row)*

A Dog on Barkham Street, by M. S. Stolz (Harper & Row, $2.95). Fear of the bully next door and longing for a dog—these were Edward's problems until the arrival of his wandering Uncle Josh with a dog that adopted Edward.

Dot for Short, by Frieda Friedman (William Morrow, $2.95; paperback, Scholastic, 50¢). The adventures of a happy family with four children, living under the old Third Avenue Elevated in New York City.

Ellen Tebbits, by Beverly Cleary (William Morrow, $2.75; paperback, Scholastic, 35¢). The adventures and crises of a little girl whose mother makes her wear long underwear even with her ballet costume. Continued in **Otis Spofford.**

The Golden Name Day, by Jennie Lindquist (Harper & Row, $2.95). How nine-year-old Nancy learned to love Swedish customs during a long stay with her grandparents in New England.

Gone-Away Lake, by Elizabeth Enright (Harcourt, Brace & World, $3.50). Julian and Portia explore a swamp that was once a lake and get to know an erratic pair who live in seclusion.

Henner's Lydia, by Marguerite de Angeli (Doubleday, $2.75). A Pennsylvania Dutch story of a little girl and her hooked rug.

Henry Huggins, by Beverly Cleary (William Morrow, $2.75; paperback, Scholastic, 35¢). The adventures of a boy who always gets into funny situations. Also **Henry and Beezus, Henry and Ribsy, Henry and the Clubhouse** and others.

Henry Reed, Inc., by Keith Robertson (Viking Press, $3). The amusing journal of an enterprising 12-year-old who sets up a research firm with the girl next door.

Herbert, by Hazel Wilson (Alfred A. Knopf, $2.75). Comical adventures of a small boy in a small town. Continued in **Herbert Again** and **Herbert's Homework.**

Homer Price, by Robert McCloskey (Viking Press, $2.75; paperback, Scholastic, 50¢). Six hilarious stories of a boy's enterprises in a small Midwestern town.

The Hundred Dresses, by Eleanor Estes (Harcourt, Brace & World, $3). A little Polish girl, teased by her classmates because she always wears the same dress, finally wins approval.

Judy's Journey, by Lois Lenski (J. B. Lippincott, $4.50). Judy is the daughter of an Alabama sharecropper, who becomes a migratory worker and follows the crops. Also **Strawberry Girl,** a story laid in rural Florida.

Katie John, by Mary Calhoun (Harper & Row, $2.95; paperback, Scholastic, 35¢). The adventures of a very independent ten-year-old, whose family has just moved to a Missouri town. Continued in **Depend on Katie John.**

The Light at Tern Rock, by Julia Sauer (Viking Press, $2.50). A boy and his aunt are stranded at a lighthouse for a memorable Christmas holiday.

Little Navajo Bluebird, by Ann Nolan Clark (Viking Press, $2.75). A present-day Navajo family of sheepherders begins to feel the impact of the outside world.

Melindy's Medal, by Georgene Faulkner and John Leonard Becker (Julian Messner, $2.75). How an eight-year-old Negro girl faces the problems that arise on her visit to the segregated South.

Miracles on Maple Hill, by Virginia Sorensen (Harcourt, Brace & World, $2.95). A family with many troubles builds a new life in the country, where neighbors and the changing seasons bring hope.

The Moffats, by Eleanor Estes (Harcourt, Brace & World, $3.25). The Moffat family—four children and Mama—have exciting times despite a limited budget. Continued in **The Middle Moffat** and **Rufus M.**

A Place for Johnny Bill, by Ruth Bishop Juline (Westminster Press, $2.95). A family of migratory workers moves from crop to crop, living in one miserable shack after the other until ten-year-old Johnny Bill helps them find a new way of life.

Plain Girl, by Virginia Sorensen (Harcourt, Brace & World, $2.75). An Amish girl who has been taught at home suddenly realizes how different the Amish life is from the world outside.

A Present from Rosita, by Celeste Edell (Julian Messner, $2.75). What happens to one little Puerto Rican girl when she comes to live in the United States.

Project Genius, by William Hayes (Atheneum, $3.25; paperback, Scholastic, 35¢). The comical story of Pete Sheldon's astonishing ideas for his school's Original Outside Project Contest.

Quiet Boy, by Lela and Rufus Waltrip (David McKay Co., $2.95).

A Navajo boy in a government school struggles to reconcile the ways of his ancestors and those of the white man.

The Saturdays, by Elizabeth Enright (Holt, Rinehart & Winston, $3). How four motherless children with the aid of their father and a housekeeper evolve a scheme for their Saturdays in New York. Also **The Four-Story Mistake** and **Then There Were Five.**

The Secret of Crossbone Hill, by Wilson Gage (World Publishing Co., $2.95). A swiftly paced mystery story laid in the South Carolina lowlands where David and Kathy Vance are vacationing.

Sensible Kate, by Doris Gates (Viking Press, $3; paperback, Scholastic, 50¢). Kate, an orphan in a foster home, longs to be pretty and cute, not just sensible.

Shaken Days, by Marion Garthwaite (Julian Messner, $2.95). The adventures of an interesting family in the days of the San Francisco earthquake and fire.

A Sundae with Judy, by Frieda Friedman (William Morrow & Co., $2.95). The heartwarming story of neighborliness in a crowded New York tenement section.

That Summer on Catalpa Street, by Louise Pliss (Reilly & Lee, $2.95). When the four Prince children moved to Catalpa Street, fun and adventures began for everyone.

This Boy Cody, by Leon Wilson (Franklin Watts, $2.95). The rollicking story of a Tennessee mountain boy who boasts he is a "ring-tailed tooter."

For better readers of 12 and up

. . . And Now Miguel, by Joseph Krumgold (Thomas Y. Crowell, $3.50). The middle son in a family of sheepherders in New Mexico longs to go to the mountains with the men of the family.

Mary Jane, by Dorothy Sterling (Doubleday, $2.95). A warmly moving story of a Negro girl who enters a newly integrated junior high school.

Meet the Austins, by Madeleine L'Engle (Vanguard, $3). The close-knit loyalty of the Austin family is threatened by the arrival of Maggy, petulant and spoiled.

My Side of the Mountain, by Jean George (E. P. Dutton, $3). The absorbing story of a New York City boy who goes to the Catskills to live on the abandoned acres of his great-grandfather. His home is a hollow in the trunk of a hemlock six feet in diameter.

Old Yeller, by Fred Gipson, (Harper & Row, $2.95; paperback, Pocket Books, 35¢). A stray dog attaches himself to a family in Texas hill country in the 1860's and defends them against wild animals and every danger.

Red Horse Hill, by Stephen Meader (Harcourt, Brace & World, $3.25). An orphan boy who is a horse lover establishes himself with a New Hampshire family and wins a cutter race.

Sea Pup, by Archie Binns (Duell, Sloan & Pearce, $3.50; paperback edition entitled *See Here, Buster!*, Scholastic, 50¢). When Clint brings home a baby seal as a pet, a beautiful friendship develops. But trouble threatens when Buster begins to grow and get out of hand.

Swamp Cat, by Jim Kjelgaard (Dodd, Mead, $3). The adventures of a boy who lives on the edge of a swamp and the black cat who shares his cabin and becomes a part of his rugged world.

The Yearling, by Marjorie Kinnan Rawlings (Charles Scribner's Sons, paperbound, $1.65). Jody Baxter's devotion to his pet fawn meets a severe test when Flag, the fawn, breaks into Ma Baxter's garden. A beautifully written story of a boy's problems in growing up.

STORIES OF ADVENTURE IN OTHER LANDS

For children from 5 to 8

Andy Says Bonjour!, by Pat Diska and Chris Jenkyns (Vanguard Press, $3). How an American boy in Paris tries to communicate with his French playmates.

Crow Boy, by Taro Yashima (Viking Press, $3). A shy little boy in a Japanese school is ridiculed by his classmates who later discover he has much to give them.

The Happy Orpheline, by Natalie Savage Carlson (Harper & Row, $3.50). A delightful tale of twenty little French girls in a down-at-the-heel orphanage. Continued in **A Brother for the Orphelines.**

A Hero by Mistake, by Anita Brenner (William R. Scott, $2.50). How Dionisio, a frightened Mexican Indian, became a brave man in spite of his fears. Very popular with all ages.

Jeanne-Marie Counts Her Sheep, by Françoise (Charles Scribner's Sons, $3.25). A little French girl and her sheep, Patapon, decide what she will buy with the wool from Patapon's lamb. Delightful surprise ending. Also **Jeanne-Marie in Gay Paris** and **Jeanne-Marie at the Fair.**

Little Baptiste, by May McNeer (Houghton Mifflin, $2.50). A small boy on a Canadian farm leads such strange animals as a pelican and a monkey out of the woods to help with the work.

Little Pear, by Eleanor Frances Lattimore (Harcourt, Brace & World, $2.95). An endearing story of a little Chinese boy who has one escapade after another.

Looking-for-Something, by Ann Nolan Clark (Viking Press, $2.75). An inquisitive little gray burro wanders from place to place in Ecuador.

Madeline, by Ludwig Bemelmans (Viking Press, $3.50). Charming story of little girls in a French school who like to do everything in unison.

My Mother Is the Most Beautiful Woman in the World, by Becky Reyher (Lothrop, Lee & Shepard, $2.50). In this old Russian folk tale, a little girl who is lost describes her mother as the most beautiful woman in the world.

Nu Dang and His Kite, by Jacqueline Ayer (Harcourt, Brace & World, $2.75). A boy in Siam loses his kite, and as he searches for it we learn fascinating things about his way of life. Lyrical text and beautiful illustrations.

Ola, by Ingri and Edgar d'Aulaire (Doubleday, $3). A beautiful and entirely childlike picture story of Norway.

Pelle's New Suit, by Elsa Beskow (Harper & Row, $2.50). How a Swedish boy earned a new suit, and how the suit was made from raw wool.

The Poppy Seed Cakes, by Margery Clark (Doubleday, $2.75). Amusing stories about Andrewshek, a little Russian boy.

Snipp, Snapp, Snurr and the Red Shoes, by Maj Lindman (Albert Whitman, $1.75). Three young Swedish boys take

From Nu Dang and His Kite, *written and illustrated by*
Jacqueline Ayer (Harcourt, Brace & World)

on jobs to earn money for their mother's birthday present. This
is a long-time favorite.

Wheel on the Chimney, by Margaret Wise Brown (J. B. Lippincott, $3). Brilliant pictures and rhythmic text tell the year-round
story of storks from a Hungarian chimney.

For children from 9 to 12

All the Proud Tribesmen, by Kylie Tennant (St Martin's Press,
$2.95). A native boy of Firecrest Island near New Guinea tells
how his people escaped just before a volcano blew their island
to bits.

Ballet Shoes, by Noel Streatfeild (Random House, $2.95). How
three English children study for careers on the London stage.
Also **Movie Shoes** and **Family Shoes.**

The Big Wave, by Pearl S. Buck (John Day, $2.97; paperback,
Scholastic, 50¢). The story of a Japanese fishing village when
a tidal wave strikes.

Boy of the Islands, by William Lipkind (Harcourt, Brace &
World, $2.75). Lua, boy of the Hawaiian Islands in ancient
times, prepares to succeed his grandfather as a tribal chief.

Boy of the Pyramids, by Ruth Fosdick Jones (Random House, $2.95). Children in ancient Egypt solve a mystery.

Burma Boy, by Willis Lindquist (McGraw-Hill, $2.75). The stirring tale of Haji's love and agonizing search for a great jungle elephant.

Call It Courage, by Armstrong Sperry (Macmillan, $2.95). Mafatu, marooned on a desert island, makes weapons and a canoe to escape and thus regains the respect of his fellow tribesmen in the South Sea islands.

A Cap for Mul Chand, by Julie Forsyth Batchelor (Harcourt, Brace & World, $2.75). How an 11-year-old boy in India earns money for a cap.

The Cheerful Heart, by Elizabeth Janet Gray (Viking Press, $3). An appealing story of an 11-year-old Japanese girl and her family who must rebuild their home and their very lives after World War II. A moving picture of family loyalty.

Chendru, the Boy and the Tiger, by Astrid Bergman Sucksdorff (Harcourt, Brace & World, $3.25). Stunning full-color photo book with interesting text about a boy in an Indian jungle village whose pet is a tiger cub.

Dog Toby, by Richard Church (John Day, $3). The heart-warming story of a boy and a dog on the border between two European countries where freedom is in peril.

The Echo Song, by Rosalie Fry (E. P. Dutton, $3.25). A warm family story which takes place in Wales where a song contest, the threat of eggs being stolen from the nest of a kite, and the restoration of an ancient woolen mill add suspense.

Eskimo Boy, by Pipaluk Freuchen (Lothrop, Lee & Shepard, $2.50). A young boy's courageous attempt to save his family from starvation after his father is killed in a walrus hunt.

The Family Under the Bridge, by Natalie Savage Carlson (Harper & Row, $3.50). Three children and their mother find shelter under one of the bridges of Paris and worm their way into the affection of a hobo who shows them Christmas in the city and finds them a real home.

Faraway Farm, by Hilda Boden (David McKay Co., $2.95). Four London children and their widowed mother move to a tiny farm in the Highlands of Scotland and make a new life for themselves.

Five Boys in a Cave, by Richard Church (John Day, $3.50). One day's adventures of English boys exploring a cave in their neighborhood bring suspense, danger and changing leadership as the boys react under stress.

Gift of the Forest, by R. Lal Singh and Eloise Lownsbery (David McKay Co., $4). A delightful story of a Hindu boy who raised a Royal Bengal tiger in rural India.

The Girl from Nowhere, by Hertha von Gebhardt (Criterion Books, $3.25). The mysterious appearance of a strange girl sitting by the lamppost stirs the other children to taunt her, build wild tales about her, and finally befriend her in this highly sensitive story first published in Germany.

The Good Master, by Kate Seredy (Viking Press, $3.50). Kate, a headstrong tomboy from Budapest, goes to live on her uncle's farm, where she learns to love and respect others.

The Happy Days, by Kim Yong Ik (Little, Brown, $3.50). A Korean orphan boy makes his way back to relatives and there takes up the struggle to earn a living, help build a school, and find "the happy days" his mother had talked about.

Heidi, by Johanna Spyri (Grosset & Dunlap, $1.95; paperbound editions, 50¢–95¢). The beloved story of a little girl whose sunny nature softened the heart of her gruff old Alm Uncle with whom she lived in the Swiss Alps.

The Horse Without a Head, by Paul Berna (Pantheon Books, $2.75). French children from the wrong side of the tracks coast down Poverty Lane on a headless, three-wheeled wooden horse and find themselves in a police court mystery.

The Jungle Book, by Rudyard Kipling (Doubleday, $3.50; paperback, New American Library, 50¢). Stories of the East Indian jungle and the boy who was adopted by a wolf pack.

The Knights of King Midas, by Paul Berna (Pantheon, $3). French boys and girls in a street gang come to the aid of elderly citizens whose shanties are burned out and who are threatened with loss of their land as well.

The Orphans of Simitra, by Paul-Jacques Bonzon (Criterion Books, $3.50). Two Greek children, made homeless orphans by an earthquake, are sent to a foster home in Holland and

then are separated and begin the long search to find each
other.

Shan's Lucky Knife, a Burmese Folk Tale, retold by Jean
Merrill (William R. Scott, $3). How a boy from the hills tricks
a sly boat master from Rangoon. A vivid picture of life on the
Irrawaddy.

"What Then, Raman?", by Shirley L. Arora (Follett Publishing
Co., $3.50). A moving story of India today as seen through
the life of a young boy, the first in his village to learn to read.
Paperback edition published by Scholastic under the title *Tiger
on the Mountain*, 45¢.

The Wheel on the School, by Meindert DeJong (Harper & Row,
$3.50). Children in a Dutch village rush to put a wheel on their
school in time for storks to build there.

For better readers of 12 and up

Avalanche!, by A. Rutgers van der Loeff (William Morrow,
$2.95). An avalanche in the Swiss Alps brings death and
destruction to the home and village of the 13-year-old hero,
who gains courage from orphan boys helping with the rescue
work.

Banner in the Sky, by James Ramsey Ullman (J. B. Lippincott,
$3.50). The thrilling story of a 16-year-old boy who rebelled
at his job as a hotel dishwasher and became a famous Alpine
climber. Paperback edition published by Pocket Books under
the title *Third Man on the Mountain*, 35¢.

Caves of the Great Hunters, by Hans Bauman (Pantheon Books,
$3.50). The true story of four boys who discovered an Ice Age
cave with its treasures of prehistoric art. Illustrated with photographs of the cave paintings.

Daughter of the Mountains, by Louise Rankin (Viking Press,
$3.25). How a Tibetan girl makes a long journey from her
mountain home to the coast of India to find her lost dog.

Devil's Hill, by Nan Chauncey (Franklin Watts, $2.95). When
Sam, a cousin from "outside," comes to visit Badge and his
family in the bush country of Tasmania, he complains about
no lights, no radio and no ham breakfast. An expedition to find
a lost heifer helps Sam learn to pull his weight and enjoy
rural life.

The House of Sixty Fathers, by Meindert DeJong (Harper & Row, $2.95). A small Chinese boy, separated from his family in time of war, makes a heroic trek back with his pet pig.

The Singing Cave, by Elís Dillon (Funk & Wagnalls, $2.95). An exciting adventure story laid on the Irish Island of Barrinish. The mystery of a missing Viking skeleton adds to the suspense.

HISTORY IN BIOGRAPHY, FICTION AND NONFICTION

For children from 5 to 8

Abraham Lincoln, by Ingri and Edgar d'Aulaire (Doubleday, $3). An introductory picture-book biography with brilliant illustrations. Also **George Washington, Benjamin Franklin** and **Buffalo Bill.**

Augustus and the River, by Le Grand (Grosset & Dunlap, $1.50). The entertaining adventures of a lively boy and his family on a Mississippi shanty boat. Continued in **Augustus Goes South, Augustus and the Mountains,** and others.

The Bears on Hemlock Mountain, by Alice Dalgliesh (Charles Scribner's Sons, $2.75). An eight-year-old sent over Hemlock Mountain to borrow an iron pot is afraid of bears on the trail and finally meets them.

Caroline and Her Kettle Named Maud, by Miriam E. Mason (Macmillan, $2.75). When Caroline's family moved to Michigan in pioneer times, she received a kettle although she wanted a gun. Later in time of crisis the kettle proved very useful. Also **Susannah, the Pioneer Cow.**

Columbus Story, by Alice Dalgliesh (Charles Scribner's Sons, $3.25). Good read-aloud story tells the life of Columbus with handsome pictures.

The Courage of Sarah Noble, by Alice Dalgliesh (Charles Scribner's Sons, $2.75). Eight-year-old Sarah goes into the Connecticut wilderness with her father in the early 1700's to take care of him while he builds a house for the family.

Dan Beard: Boy Scout, by Miriam E. Mason (Bobbs-Merrill, $2.25). A simply-written biography in the Childhood of Famous Americans series.

Inside the iron pot
it was dark, and Jonathan was
far from comfortable.

From The Bears on Hemlock Mountain, *By Alice
Dalgliesh, illustrated by Helen Sewell (Charles Scribner's
Sons)*

Down the Mississippi, by Clyde Robert Bulla (Thomas Y. Crowell, $2.95; paperback, Scholastic, 50¢). A farm boy's adventures on the Mississippi in pioneer days.

Florence Nightingale: War Nurse, by Anne Colver (Garrard Publishing Co., $2.25). A simple and pleasing biography for second and third graders.

George Washington Carver, by Sam and Beryl Epstein (Garrard Publishing Co., $2.25). An easy biography for the youngest readers.

Look Out for Pirates!, by Iris Vinton (Random House, $1.95). An exciting book for beginning readers, written with only 177 different words.

Pilgrim Thanksgiving, by Wilma Pitchford Hays (Coward-McCann, $2.75). A little girl's experiences and reactions on the first Thanksgiving Day.

Riding the Pony Express, by Clyde Robert Bulla (Thomas Y. Crowell, $2.95; paperback, Scholastic, 45¢). The son of a Pony Express rider has to pinch-hit for his father in a crisis.

The Thanksgiving Story, by Alice Dalgliesh (Charles Scribner's Sons, $3.25). A simply-written story of the first year in the Plymouth Colony.

For children from 9 to 12

Abe Lincoln Gets His Chance, by Francis Cavanah (Rand McNally, $3.50; paperback, Scholastic, 35¢). A warm fictionalized story of Lincoln's life before becoming President.

The Adventures of Tom Sawyer, by Mark Twain (Grosset & Dunlap, $1.95; paperbound editions, 45¢–95¢). A perennial favorite of boys and girls.

All-of-a-Kind Family, by Sydney Taylor (Follett Publishing Co., $3.50). Five little daughters of a Jewish junk dealer in New York's lower East Side in the early 1900's manage to have a lively time with little money.

America Is Born, by Gerald W. Johnson (William Morrow, $3.95). The first of a three-volume history of the United States for children—vivid, dramatic, authoritative and beautifully illustrated. The other two: **America Grows Up** and **America Moves Forward.**

America's Robert E. Lee, by Henry Steele Commager and Lynd Ward (Houghton Mifflin, $3.75). A vivid account of the life of the Confederate general, beautifully illustrated.

Antelope Singer, by Ruth M. Underhill (Coward-McCann, $3.50). When 10-year-old Tad's father becomes ill from snake-bite on the way to California with a covered wagon train, they are befriended by Paiute Indians and spend the winter with them.

Away Goes Sally, by Elizabeth Coatsworth (Macmillan, $3). Quaint story of a family that moves to Maine in a little house on runners drawn over the snow by oxen. Good details of life of early settlers. Continued in **Five Bushel Farm, The White Horse,** and other books.

Ben and Me, by Robert Lawson (Little, Brown, $3). The humorous life history of Benjamin Franklin as told by his good mouse Amos.

Benjamin West and His Cat Grimalkin, by Marguerite Henry and Wesley Dennis (Bobbs-Merrill, $3.50). How a Quaker lad in colonial Pennsylvania followed the suggestions of his cat and became a great painter.

Blanche of the Blueberry Barrens, by Anne Molloy (Hastings House, $2.95). In the summer of 1917 10-year-old Blanche learns to assume responsibilities while others in the family go out to rake blueberries in Maine.

Bronco Charlie: Rider of the Pony Express, by Henry V. Larom (McGraw-Hill, $2.75; paperback, Scholastic, 35¢). The true story of a boy rider with the Pony Express.

Buffalo Kill, by Gardell Dano Christensen (Thomas Nelson & Sons, $2.95). The 12-year-old son of a medicine chief of prehistoric Great Plains Indians leads a herd of buffalo over the cliff for slaughter by the tribe.

The Building of the First Transcontinental Railroad, by Adele Gutman Nathan (Random House, $1.95). A colorful and dramatic chapter in the opening of the West.

The Cabin Faced West, by Jean Fritz (Coward-McCann, $3; paperback, Scholastic, 35¢). Excellent story of a little girl in the pioneer days of western Pennsylvania.

Caddie Woodlawn, by Carol Ryrie Brink (Macmillan, $3.50; paperback, Macmillan, 79¢). Tomboy Caddie and her brothers have many exciting adventures on the Wisconsin frontier of the 1860's.

Children of the Red King, by Madeleine Polland (Holt, Rinehart & Winston, $3). The time is 1209. The place is Ireland, where the children of the Red King of Connacht help to save their father after the Norman Conquest.

Christmas on the Mayflower, by Wilma Pitchford Hays (Coward-McCann, $2.75). The Pilgrims' first Christmas in the New World was spent on the *Mayflower* just off Cape Cod with the men ashore working on the first building and the crew threatening mutiny.

The Colorado, Mover of Mountains, by Alexander L. Crosby (Garrard Publishing Co., $2.50). A fascinating report of the exploration of the river and its dramatic history.

Custer's Last Stand, by Quentin Reynolds (Random House, $1.95). An exciting and bitter chapter in American history.

Dollar for Luck, by Elizabeth Coatsworth (Macmillan, $3). A boy and girl on the coast of Maine in 1882 have adventures on a schooner with a dollar on its mast.

The Door in the Wall, by Marguerite de Angeli (Doubleday, $3.50). Robin, a 10-year-old boy, is crippled by illness during the plague in thirteenth-century England, but wins the right to knighthood.

The Far Frontier, by William O. Steele (Harcourt, Brace & World, $2.95). When Tobe, the son of an illiterate backwoodsman, is bound out to a naturalist searching the woods for plant and animal life he learns the meaning of loyalty and develops appreciation for learning.

The First Year, by Enid Meadowcroft (Thomas Y. Crowell, $2.95). Life on the *Mayflower* and in Plymouth during the Pilgrims' first year.

George Washington, by Genevieve Foster (Charles Scribner's Sons, $2.95). An interesting, well-illustrated biography. Also **Abraham Lincoln.**

Hitty: Her First Hundred Years, by Rachel Field (Macmillan, $3). The autobiography of a doll carved from a block of mountain ash—a doll which has had an exciting and varied career.

Little House in the Big Woods, by Laura Ingalls Wilder (Harper

& Row, $2.95). The author's childhood eighty years ago on the edge of the Big Woods in Wisconsin. Continued in **Little House on the Prairie, Farmer Boy, On the Banks of Plum Creek** and **By the Shores of Silver Lake.**

Mark Twain and the River, by Sterling North (Houghton Mifflin, $1.95). A biography that reflects the mood and flavor of Mark Twain's own books.

Martha, Daughter of Virginia, by Marguerite Vance (E. P. Dutton, $3.25). History and romance combine in this biography of Martha Washington.

The Matchlock Gun, by Walter D. Edmonds (Dodd, Mead, $2.95). With an old matchlock gun a young boy holds off an Indian raid.

Mr. Revere and I, by Robert Lawson (Little, Brown, $3.75). The life of Paul Revere as told by his famous horse.

Paddle-to-the-Sea, by Holling C. Holling (Houghton Mifflin, $3.75). The journey of a tiny canoe, launched by an Indian boy, reveals the dangers of travel through the Great Lakes and the St. Lawrence to the Atlantic.

The Pony Express, by Samuel Hopkins Adams (Random House, $1.95). Historical information is presented with all the excitement and suspense of pioneer days.

Ride on the Wind, by Alice Dalgliesh (Charles Scribner's Sons, $3.25). An adaptation of Lindbergh's **The Spirit of St. Louis** with dramatic action and poetic quality.

The Rise and Fall of Adolf Hitler, by William L. Shirer (Random House, $1.95). Simply written, accurate account of Hitler and Nazism.

The Sinking of the Bismarck, by William L. Shirer (Random House, $1.95). A vivid and dramatic chapter in the history of World War II.

Snow Treasure, by Marie McSwigan (E. P. Dutton, $3.50; paperback, Scholastic, 50¢). How Norwegian children during the Nazi occupation got blocks of gold out of the country.

Stories California Indians Told, by Anne B. Fisher (Parnassus Press, $2.95). Indian legends that explain how California was made, how the earthquakes began, how a rainbow was born, etc.

Sunrise Island, by Charlotte Baker (David McKay Co., $3.25).

Adventures of two Indian boys in a tribe of the Northwest
Coast many years ago.

The Swamp Fox, by Marion Marsh Brown (Westminster Press,
$2.95). Fictionalized biography of Francis Marion, leader of
Revolutionary War guerillas who harassed the British from
the swamps of South Carolina.

Ten and a Kid, by Sadie Rose Weilerstein (Doubleday, $2.95).
A warmly convincing story of a family in a small Jewish town
of Lithuania before the First World War.

Thee, Hannah!, by Marguerite de Angeli (Doubleday, $2.95).
A lively tale of a little Quaker girl in old Philadelphia.

Thomas Jefferson, Champion of the People, by Clara Ingram
Judson (Follett Publishing Co., $3.50). The highly readable
life story of a man whose ideas are much discussed today. Also
Theodore Roosevelt, Fighting Patriot and **Abraham Lincoln,
Friend of the People.**

Three Without Fear, by Robert C. Du Soe (David McKay Co.,
$3.25). A boy shipwrecked off the coast of Lower California
drifts ashore and meets two Indian children. Together they
have a perilous journey to safety.

Trail to Oklahoma, by Jim Booker (Broadman Press, $2.95).
The gripping story of a 12-year-old Indian boy and his family
on the forced march of the Cherokees from North Carolina to
Oklahoma.

Twenty and Ten, by Claire Huchet Bishop (Viking Press, $2.50).
Twenty French children risk everything during World War II
to shelter ten Jewish refugee children.

The Winged Watchman, by Hilda van Stockum (Farrar, Straus
& Co., $3.25). A Dutch family during the German occupa-
tion of World War II shows quiet heroism in the resistance
movement.

Winter Danger, by William O. Steele (Harcourt, Brace & World,
$2.50). After wandering the woods with his father, Jared has
difficulty settling down in a frontier village of Tennessee. Also
The Lone Hunt and **Daniel Boone's Echo.**

Yonie Wondernose, by Marguerite de Angeli (Doubleday, $2.75).
The amusing story of a Pennsylvania Dutch boy whose curiosity
was never satisfied. Also **Skippack School** and **Henner's
Lydia.**

For better readers of 12 and up

The Adventures of Huckleberry Finn, by Mark Twain (Grosset & Dunlap, $1.95; 12 paperbound editions, 45¢–$1.32). A thrilling adventure story that children love.

The Ark, by Margot Benary-Isbert (Harcourt, Brace & World, $3.25). A modern German family in a bombed-out city makes a new beginning in West Germany. Continued in **Rowan Farm.**

The Bearcat, by Annabel and Edgar Johnson (Harper & Row, $3.50). After failing the eighth grade, Jeff goes to work in the Bearcat Mine in Montana at the turn of the century where he learns the bitter facts about low wages, unsafe working conditions, and the tyranny of the company store.

Bowleg Bill: Seagoing Cowpuncher, by Harold W. Felton (Prentice-Hall, $2.95). The tall tale of a Wyoming cowhand who rode a Yankee clipper instead of a cow pony and roped tuna instead of a steer.

Brady, by Jean Fritz (Coward-McCann, $3.50). The story of a boy in pre-Civil War days who makes up his mind on the slavery issue and helps his father in the underground railroad.

Calico Captive, by Elizabeth George Speare (Houghton Mifflin, $3.50). The adventures of Miriam Willard who was captured with her family in an Indian raid in New Hampshire in 1754.

Carry On, Mr. Bowditch, by Jean Lee Latham (Houghton Mifflin, $3.25). An absorbing biography of a young boy who mastered the secrets of navigation by himself and became famous in marine history.

Danger to Windward, by Armstrong Sperry, (Holt, Rinehart & Winston, $2.95). An exciting story of whaling adventures in Nantucket following the War of 1812.

Daniel Boone, by James Daugherty (Viking Press, $4). Illustrated life story of the rugged pioneer, told with gusto.

The Diary of a Young Girl, by Anne Frank (Pocket Books, paperbound, 35¢). Humor, pathos and tragedy are intermingled in this day-by-day record of a young Jewish girl who with her family is hiding from the Nazi secret police.

Harriet Tubman: Conductor on the Underground Railroad,

by Ann Petry (Thomas Y. Crowell, $3.50). About the Negro leader, born a slave, who escaped by the underground railroad and led three hundred others to safety.

Johnny Tremain, by Esther Forbes (Houghton Mifflin, $3.50; paperback, Houghton Mifflin, $1.32). A moving story of a silversmith's apprentice in Boston at the time of Paul Revere. Although the hero is a teen-ager, his story appeals to younger boys as well.

Little Women, by Louisa May Alcott (Thomas Y. Crowell, $3.50; 4 paperback editions, 50¢–95¢). The favorite story of the author's childhood in a family of four girls.

Mary McLeod Bethune, by Emma Gelders Sterne (Alfred A. Knopf, $3.50). A sensitively written biography of the great Negro leader whose childhood in a poverty-stricken area of the South helped her understand the needs of other young people.

The Ordeal of the Young Hunter, by Jonreed Lauritzen (Little, Brown, $3). How a young Navajo boy becomes a hero and learns to understand his own people.

Out of the Mines, The Story of a Pit Boy, by Frederick Grice (Franklin Watts, $2.95). The gripping story of a 12-year-old English boy who goes to work in the mines with his father and brother, then rebels against the misery of mine life.

The Quest of Isaac Newton, by Barbara and Myrick Land (Doubleday, $2.50). A lively, highly readable biography with a very modern look.

Railroads in the Days of Steam, by Albert L. McCready (American Heritage Publishing Co., $3.95). A fascinating history of American railroads illustrated by old prints, photos and drawings.

The Silver Sword, by Ian Serraillier (Criterion, $3.50; paperback edition published by Scholastic under the title *Escape from Warsaw*, 35¢). A moving story of Polish children separated from their parents when the Germans took over in World War II and the long journey to Switzerland in the hope of reunion.

The Story of D-Day: June 6, 1944, by Bruce Bliven, Jr. (Random House, $1.95). A vivid account of the Allied landing in France during World War II.

Thirty Seconds Over Tokyo, by Bob Considine and Ted Lawson (Random House, $1.95). First-hand report of American bombing of Japan in World War II.

Throw Stone, by E. B. Sayles and Mary Ellen Stevens (Reilly and Lee, $3.75). For the good reader interested in prehistoric times, this is an excellent story of the first American boy 25,000 years ago, as written by a noted anthropologist.

The Wonderful Winter, by Marchette Chute (E. P. Dutton, $3.50). The story of a young boy who spends the winter in the London home of a great actor in Shakespeare's day.

Young Fu of the Upper Yangtze, by Elizabeth Foreman Lewis (Holt, Rinehart & Winston, $3.95). The adventures of a Chinese boy from the country who goes to live in the city.

FAIRY TALES, FOLK TALES AND LEGENDS

Anansi the Spider Man, by Philip M. Sherlock (Thomas Y. Crowell, $3.50). Jamaican folk tales about Anansi, who was both man and spider, and his animal friends. Fine for reading aloud.

The Arabian Nights, edited by Andrew Lang (David McKay Co., $3.50). Such popular tales as "Aladdin," "Ali Baba and the Forty Thieves" and "Sinbad the Sailor."

The Blue Fairy Book, collected and edited by Andrew Lang David McKay Co., $3.50). Tales from many lands, including folk tales and legends.

Castles and Dragons, Read-to-Yourself Fairy Tales for Boys and Girls, compiled by the Child Study Association of America (Thomas Y. Crowell, $3.95). These 18 fairy stories by distinguished modern authors abound in brave heroes, beautiful heroines and magic.

The Cow-Tail Switch and Other West African Stories, by Harold Courlander and George Herzog (Holt, Rinehart & Winston, $3.50). Wise and humorous tales gathered from native storytellers.

East of the Sun and West of the Moon, by Peter Asbjørnsen (Macmillan, $2.95). Norwegian folk tales including such favorites as "Three Billy Goats Gruff" and "The Giant Who Had No Heart in His Body."

English Fairy Tales, by Joseph Jacobs (G. P. Putnam's Sons, $2.95). "Jack and the Beanstalk," "Dick Whittington and His Cat" and 40 other tales retold for all ages.

Fairy Tales, by Hans Christian Andersen (Grosset & Dunlap, $1.95). Timeless favorites illustrated by Arthur Szyk.

Favorite Fairy Tales Told in England, retold by Virginia Haviland (Little, Brown, $2.95). Six wonderful stories retold for children to read to themselves about such well-known characters as Tom Thumb, Dick Whittington, and Johnny-cake. Also, **Favorite Fairy Tales Told in France, Told in Germany, Told in Norway, Told in Russia.**

Favorite Stories Old and New, selected by Sidonie M. Gruenberg (Doubleday, $3.95). A big collection of favorite stories of all kinds.

The Golden Phoenix, by Marius Barbeau (Henry Z. Walck, $3). Eight French-Canadian fairy tales, beautifully illustrated and excellent for reading aloud.

The Gorgon's Head, the Story of Perseus, by Ian Serraillier (Henry Z. Walck, $2.95). Dramatic retelling of the old Greek legend.

Heather and Broom, Tales of the Scottish Highlands, by Sorche Nic Leodhas (Holt, Rinehart & Winston, $3.25). Stories of magic and romance that are well suited for reading aloud.

Holiday Storybook, compiled by the Child Study Association of America (Thomas Y. Crowell, $3.95). Interesting stories and verses about holidays celebrated in America.

Just So Stories, by Rudyard Kipling (Grosset & Dunlap, $1.95). Marvelous read-aloud stories that tell how the camel got his hump, how the elephant got his trunk, how the kangaroo got his long tail, and so on.

The King's Drum and Other African Stories, by Harold Courlander (Harcourt, Brace & World, $2.95). A stirring collection of tales.

The Merry Adventures of Robin Hood, by Howard Pyle (Grosset & Dunlap, $1.95). Robin Hood and his stalwart men in Sherwood Forest, who oppose the greedy and right the wrongs of the poor, are extremely popular with children.

Mike Fink, by James Cloyd Bowman (Little, Brown, $3). A master storyteller reports on the tall-tale hero whom river-men called "the snapping turtle of the O-hi-o-o and snag of the Massassip."

The Moon Is a Crystal Ball, by Natalia Belting (Bobbs-Merrill, $2.95). Folk tales that explain the sun, the moon and the stars.

Ol' Paul, the Mighty Logger, by Glen Rounds (Holiday House, $2.75). Roaring humor and frank horseplay prevail in this collection of tall tales about Paul Bunyan, the legendary super-lumberjack.

Once the Hodja, by Alice Geer Kelsey (David McKay Co., $2.95). Delightfully humorous folk tales from Turkey.

Once-upon-a-Time Story Book, edited by Rose Dobbs (Random House, $1). Old fables and tales retold for young children.

Pecos Bill, Texas Cowpuncher, by Harold W. Felton (Alfred A. Knopf, $3.09). A rousing tall tale of the legendary hero.

Pepper and Salt, by Howard Pyle (Harper & Row, $2.95). Eight humorous tales with gay verses and drawings. Also, **Wonder Clock,** a collection of old folk tales and legends.

The Raggle Taggle Fellow, by Miriam Schlein (Abelard-Schuman, $2.95). With the rhythm and wisdom of an old folk tale, this story tells how Dick, the youngest son, wins friends and good fortune with only his guitar to help him.

Read to Me Again, compiled by the Child Study Association of America (Thomas Y. Crowell, $2.95). A choice collection of wise and witty stories and verses for children under seven.

Read-to-Me Storybook, by the Child Study Association of America (Thomas Y. Crowell, $2.95). Favorite stories and poems to read to young children.

Stone Soup, by Marcia Brown (Charles Scribner's Sons, $3.25). Retelling of a humorous old tale about soup made from stones plus carrots, cabbage, meat and all the rest.

Stories of the Gods and Heroes, by Sally Benson (Dial Press, $3). The tales of the Trojan War skillfully retold.

Tales from Grimm, translated by Wanda Gág (Coward-McCann, $3.50). Delightful retelling of favorite fairy tales.

The Talking Cat and Other Stories of French Canada, by Nat-

From The Gorgon's Head, the Story of Perseus, *by Ian Serraillier, illustrated by William Stobbs (Henry Z. Walck, Inc.)*

alie Savage Carlson (Harper & Row, $2.95). Amusing animal stories and tales of adventure.

Talking Tree: Fairy Tales from 15 Lands, selected by Augusta Baker (J. B. Lippincott, $3). Twenty-eight fairy tales popular with children.

Tall Tales from the High Hills, by Ellis Credle (Thomas Nelson, $2.75). Twenty lively folk tales of the Blue Ridge Mountains. Ideal for reading aloud and storytelling.

The 397th White Elephant, by René Guillot (Criterion, $2.75). A long-ago fable from India of a Child King and the Imperial White Elephant Hong-Mo. Splendid for reading aloud.

Time for Fairy Tales, Old and New, compiled by May Hill Arbuthnot (Scott, Foresman, $5.25). A bumper collection of folk tales, myths, epics, fables and modern fanciful tales.

Told Under the Green Umbrella, by the Association for Childhood Education International (Macmillan, $3.50). Twenty-six folk tales retold for young children.

Treasured Tales: Great Stories of Faith and Courage, compiled by Laura E. Cathon and Thusnelda Schmidt (Abingdon Press, $3.50). A splendid collection of stories and poems with a nottoo-obvious moral.

The Wonder Book, by Nathaniel Hawthorne (E. P. Dutton, $2.75). Retelling of old Greek tales that have delighted children for generations. Also published with **The Tanglewood Tales** (Doubleday, paperback, 95¢).

RELIGION, BIBLE STORIES AND CHRISTMAS

Amahl and the Night Visitors, by Gian-Carlo Menotti, adapted by Frances Frost (McGraw-Hill, $3.50). Beautifully illustrated story based on the television opera of the crippled boy who sees the Three Wise Men at Christmas. (The opera is available in a recording with printed libretto.)

The Animals' Christmas, edited by Anne Thaxter Eaton (Viking Press, $2.75). Poems and stories relating the Christmas legend to animals.

Baboushka and the Three Kings, by Ruth Robbins (Parnassus Press, $2.50). An old Russian tale of the woman who was too busy to join the three kings in search of the Child but ever since has tried to follow them.

Bible Story for Boys and Girls: Old Testament ($3.50) and **Bible Story for Boys and Girls: New Testament** ($3.50) by Walter Russell Bowie (Abingdon Press). Retold in modern language with reverence and simplicity.

The Christ Child; From the Gospels According to Matthew and Luke, illustrated by Maud and Miska Petersham (Doubleday, $3). Exquisite pictures for text from the Gospels of Matthew and Luke.

The Christmas Book of Legends and Stories, edited by Elva S. Smith and Alice I. Hazeltine (Lothrop, Lee & Shepard, $3.95). A splendid collection.

David, from the story told in the First Book of Samuel and the First Book of Kings illustrated by Maud and Miska Petersham (Macmillan, $2.50). A beautifully illustrated version of the Bible story. Other books in the same series: **Joseph, Moses** and **Ruth.**

The Night Before Christmas, by Clement Clarke Moore (Grosset & Dunlap, $1). This gay story-poem should be part of every child's Christmas. Beautifully illustrated by Leonard Weisgard.

One God: The Ways We Worship Him, by Florence Mary Fitch (Lothrop, Lee & Shepard, $3). Religious observances and ways of worship of Catholics, Protestants and Jews. Also, **Allah, the God of Islam** and **Their Search for God, Ways of Worship in the Orient.**

Told Under the Christmas Tree, compiled by the Association for Childhood Education International (Macmillan, $3.50). Stories and poems about Christmas in many lands and about Hanukkah, the Jewish Festival of Lights.

SCIENCE, NATURE AND OTHER INFORMATION

Plants and Animals

For children from 5 to 8

All About Eggs and How They Change into Animals, by Millicent E. Selsam (William R. Scott, $2.75). Simple story of animal reproduction.

The Butterflies Come, by Leo Politi (Charles Scribner's Sons, $3.25). A beautifully illustrated picture story about the annual migration of the monarch butterflies.

Catch a Cricket, by Carla Stevens (William R. Scott, $3). About the capture and care of earthworms, crickets, fireflies, grasshoppers "and other companionable creatures," with excellent photographs for every step.

Deer in the Snow, by Miriam Schlein (Abelard-Schuman, $2.75). An easy-to-read story of a family that feeds deer through the hard winter. Delightful picture of the changing seasons and real feeling for wildlife.

Here Come the Raccoons! by Alice E. Goudey (Charles Scribner's Sons, $2.75). A simply written life-cycle story. Also, **Here Come the Elephants!, Here Come the Beavers!, Here Come the Deer!**

Houses from the Sea, by Alice E. Goudey (Charles Scribner's Sons, $3.25). The beautifully poetic story of finding sea shells and identifying them. Ideal to read aloud to young children.

I Like Caterpillars, by Gladys Conklin (Holiday House, $2.95). A nature picture book about the appearance and habits of many kinds of caterpillars.

Let's Go Outdoors, by Harriet E. Huntington (Doubleday, $3). Photographs and brief text tell of snails, turtles, ants, bees, polliwogs, caterpillars, etc. Also **Let's Go to the Seashore.**

Sandpipers, by Edith Thacher Hurd (Thomas Y. Crowell, $2.50). Beautifully simple text and illustrations make this a delightful informational book for the very young.

Seeds and More Seeds, by Millicent E. Selsam (Harper & Row, $1.95). A charming book that includes information, suggestions for science activities and a slight story for beginning readers.

Travelers All, the Story of How Plants Go Places, by Irma Webber (William R. Scott, $2.50). How plants travel—by sticker, by air, by water, etc.

The Tree on the Road to Turntown, by Glenn O. Blough (McGraw-Hill, $2.75). This story of the growth and development of a familiar old tree will sharpen observation and stir curiosity in a child.

The True Book of Baby Animals, by Illa Podendorf (Childrens Press, $2.00). Simple information that is intriguing to young children.

We Like Bugs, by Gladys Conklin (Holiday House, $2.95). A book for beginners which is well illustrated.

What's Inside?, by May Garelick (William R. Scott, $2.50). Photos and text give the step-by-step progress of a baby gosling as it breaks through its shell.

For children from 9 to 12

All About Dinosaurs, by Roy Chapman Andrews (Random House, $1.95). A vivid report by the world-famous scientist who discovered dinosaur eggs in the Gobi Desert.

All About Snakes, by Bessie M. Hecht (Random House, $1.95). Good information, well organized and beautifully illustrated.

All About Us, by Eva Knox Evans (Golden Press, $3.95). A simple explanation of why people look and act the way they do, their beginnings, their wanderings over the earth, and the resultant changes in skin color, customs and language.

All on a Mountain Day, by Aileen Fisher (Thomas Nelson, $2.75). Stories of nine animals whose paths cross during a June day in the Rockies.

Animal Homes, by George F. Mason (William Morrow, $2.60). Where different animals live, raise their young and store food. Also **Animal Tracks.**

A Baby Is Born, the Story of How Life Begins, by Milton Levine and Jean H. Seligmann (Golden Press, $1.99). A clear explanation, with beautiful illustrations.

Before and After Dinosaurs, by Lois and Louis Darling (William Morrow, $2.95). Good information and excellent illustrations.

Birds and Their Nests, by Olive L. Earle (William Morrow, $2.78). Clear pictures and text describe 42 varieties of birds, their nesting areas, nests, eggs, etc. Also **Crickets.**

Caterpillars, by Dorothy Sterling (Doubleday, $2.75). The life cycles, feeding habits and living place of many different species of moths and butterflies are described with accuracy and beauty.

Close-Up of a Honeybee, by Virgil E. Foster (William R. Scott, $3). Dramatic story of the author's first interest in honeybees and how he learned more about them, with excellent photographs.

Collecting Cocoons, by Lois J. Hussey and Catherine Pessino (Thomas Y. Crowell, $3). Where to find cocoons, how to collect them and the four stages they go through.

Dinosaurs, by Herbert S. Zim (William Morrow, $2.78). Good information and clear illustrations about a favorite subject of children.

The Hole in the Tree, by Jean George (E. P. Dutton, $2.75). How the hole in the apple tree is made larger by a succession of occupants and carefully watched by children who think of it as their treasure hole.

How and Why Wonder Book of Ants and Bees, by Ronald N. Rood (Grosset & Dunlap, $1). Interesting facts with good illustrations.

In Woods and Fields, by Margaret Waring Buck (Abingdon Press, $3). An ideal nature book for beginners, describing plant and animal life in various habitats at various seasons.

Insects in Their World, by Su Zan Noguchi Swain (Doubleday, $2.95). Authentic information and exquisite illustrations give the scientific explanation of insects and their ways. Good details on how to identify insects and collect them.

Junior Book of Insects, by Edwin Way Teale (E. P. Dutton, $3.75). Interesting facts about the lives and habits of the common insects with suggestions for collecting and studying them.

From See Through the Forest, *by Millicent E. Selsam,*
illustrated by Winifred Lubell (Harper & Row)

Monarch Butterfly, by Marion W. Marcher (Holiday House, $2.50). Life cycle of the monarch with beautiful illustrations.

Nature Detective, by Millicent E. Selsam (William R. Scott, $3.25). A fascinating explanation of ways to detect which animals went where, what they did and sometimes what they ate.

Prehistoric World, by Carroll Lane Fenton (John Day, $3.50). Stories of animal life in prehistoric times.

See Through the Forest, by Millicent E. Selsam (Harper & Row, $2.75). Beautifully written and illustrated report on the different floors of the forest and the plants and animals to be found in each. Also, **See Through the Lake,** by Millicent E. Selsam and Betty Morrow, and **See Up the Mountain,** by Betty Morrow.

Sixty Million Years of Horses, by Lois and Louis Darling (William Morrow, $2.75). Accurate information and illustrations about a favorite subject.

Snakes, by Herbert S. Zim (William Morrow, $2.78; paperback, Scholastic, 35¢). Facts about snakes in North America. Also **Birds, Elephants, Owls,** and many more.

Song of the Seasons, by Addison Webb (William Morrow, $3). The year-round doings of familiar woodland animals.

Strange Plants and Their Ways, by Ross E. Hutchins (Rand McNally, $3.50). A fascinating report of plants which are cannibals, robbers, parasites and travelers, with excellent photographs by the author.

The Tale of a Meadow, by Henry B. Kane (Alfred A. Knopf, $3). Beautifully written account of the author's acquaintance with the plant and animal life of a meadow, with photographs and drawings. Also, **The Tale of a Pond.**

The Sun, the Stars and Outer Space

For children from 5 to 8

A Book of Moon Rockets for You, by Franklyn M. Branley (Thomas Y. Crowell, $3.50). Accurate information that can be read by most second graders. Also **A Book of Satellites for You.**

The Day We Saw the Sun Come Up, by Alice E. Goudey (Charles Scribner's Sons, $3.25). An exquisite picture book which inspires wonder and curiosity while giving valuable information.

Junior Science Book of Stars, by Phoebe Crosby (Garrard Publishing Co., $2.25). Splendid informational book well illustrated for second and third graders.

The Moon Seems to Change, by Franklyn M. Branley (Thomas Y. Crowell, $2.50). Accurate scientific information for first and second graders is presented simply and dramatically.

Rockets Into Space, by Alexander L. Crosby and Nancy Larrick (Random House, $1.95). Simple explanation of rockets and how they work and the possibilities for space travel.

When I Go to the Moon, by Claudia Lewis (Macmillan, $3). A child's eye view of the earth from the moon.

You Among the Stars, by Herman and Nina Schneider (William R. Scott, $3.25). Elementary book of astronomy.

You and Space Travel, by John Lewellen (Childrens Press, $2). Simple explanation of the workings of the airplane propeller, helicopter, jet plane and rocket.

You Will Go to the Moon, by Mae and Ira Freeman (Random House, $1.95). The story of a trip to the moon by three-stage rocket, written for beginning readers.

For children from 9 to 12

Exploring by Satellite, by Franklyn M. Branley (Thomas Y. Crowell, $3.50). How a satellite is constructed and launched, how it maintains its orbit and how it is used in scientific research.

Exploring Mars, by Roy Gallant (Doubleday, $2.50). A readable, lavishly illustrated account of our neighbor planet. Also, **Exploring the Moon.**

Find the Constellations, by H. A. Rey (Houghton Mifflin, $3.50). How to recognize the constellations and enjoy them.

The Golden Book of Astronomy, by Rose Wyler and Gerald Ames (Golden Press, $3.99). A lavishly illustrated giant book that gives the most pertinent information about the moon, the stars, the planets, and their relationships.

Lodestar: Rocket Ship to Mars, by Franklyn M. Branley (Thomas Y. Crowell, $3.50). Good information—well written and well organized—about a subject that fascinates boys and girls. The author is Associate Astronomer at the Hayden Planetarium.

Picture Book of Astronomy, by Jerome S. Meyer (Lothrop, Lee & Shepard, $1.95). An imaginative introduction to the subject.

Science in Other Areas

For children from 5 to 8

All Around You, by Jeanne Bendick (McGraw-Hill, $3). A science picture book that tells the why and how of the world around us—wind, rain, sun, shadows and all the rest.

Busy Water, by Irma S. Black (Holiday House, $2.75). A simple report on how water keeps busy as rain, river, ocean, cloud and as rain again.

Fast Is Not a Ladybug, by Miriam Schlein (William R. Scott, $2.75). Words and pictures tell of different kinds of speed and what they can mean to a child.

I Want to Be a Scientist, by Carla Greene (Childrens Press, $2). A good introduction for children just learning to read.

Junior Science Book of Rain, Hail, Sleet and Snow, by Nancy Larrick (Garrard Publishing Co., $2.25; paperback, Scholastic, 35¢). Information about the weather for second and third graders.

Junior Science Book of Rock Collecting, by Phoebe Crosby (Garrard Publishing Co., $2.25). Good background information and specific how-to-do-it suggestions for the beginning rock collector.

Let's Find Out About Electricity, by Martha and Charles Shapp (Franklin Watts, $1.95). An easy-to-read science book which uses only one hundred different words. Also **Let's Find Out About Wheels** and **Let's Find Out About Animal Homes.**

Not Only for Ducks—The Story of Rain, by Glenn O. Blough (McGraw-Hill, $2.95). A scientific explanation of rain.

Now I Know, by Julius Schwartz (McGraw-Hill, $2.75). A clear explanation of sound, sight and feelings for the primary-school child.

Rusty Rings a Bell, by Franklyn M. Branley and Eleanor K. Vaughan (Thomas Y. Crowell, $2.50). Very easy science in narrative form.

See for Yourself, by Nancy Larrick (E. P. Dutton, $2.78). Easy science experiments with air, water and heat.

The Storm Book, by Charlotte Zolotow (Harper & Row, $2.95). Poetic prose and exquisite pictures describe a summer storm sweeping over the city, the countryside and the seashore.

Your Wonderful World of Science, by Mae and Ira Freeman (Random House, $1.95). Scientific information about air, heat, cold, rocks, water, evaporation and condensation, rain, fog, snow.

For children from 9 to 12

The Arctic Tundra, by Delia Goetz (William Morrow, $2.75). Interesting information about geography, weather, plants, animals, with many illustrations.

Birth of an Island, by Millicent E. Selsam (Harper & Row, $2.75; paperback, Scholastic, 35¢). Excellent explanation with fine illustrations.

Everyday Weather and How It Works, by Herman Schneider (McGraw-Hill, $3.25). Readable text and many lively illustrations make this a popular explanation of weather phenomena and forecasting.

Exploring the Weather, by Roy Gallant (Doubleday & Co., $2.50). Fascinating information with lavish illustrations.

The First Book of Measurement, by Sam and Beryl Epstein (Franklin Watts, $1.95). A lively explanation that is full of interesting information.

The First Book of Stones, by M. B. Cormack (Franklin Watts, $1.95). Excellent for the young collector who must know why as well as how.

How Atomic Submarines Are Made, by David C. Cooke (Dodd, Mead, $2.50). Words and photographs tell how the first atomic submarine was made and how those of the future will be built.

Hurricanes and Twisters, by Robert Irving (Alfred A. Knopf, $3; paperback, Scholastic, 50¢). Photographs and easy text explain how hurricanes originate, operate and travel.

It's Fun to Know Why: Experiments With Things Around Us, by Julius Schwartz (McGraw-Hill, $2.75). Simple experiments that explain such everyday materials as iron, coal, cement, glass, rubber, salt, bread, soap and paper.

Let's Find Out, by Nina and Herman Schneider (William R. Scott, $2.75; paperback, Scholastic, 35¢). Simple science experiments with air, heat and water.

Let's Look Under the City, by Herman and Nina Schneider (William R. Scott, $2.50). A description of water, gas, electricity and telephone carriers under the city streets. Also **Let's Look Inside Your House.**

Lightning and Thunder, by Herbert S. Zim (William Morrow, $2.78). An explanation of lightning and thunder with suggested activities to help understand static electricity.

One Hundred and One Science Experiments, by Illa Podendorf (Grosset & Dunlap, $3.95). An excellent collection for parents to use with their children.

Rocks and Their Stories, by Carroll Lane Fenton and Mildred A. Fenton (Doubleday, $2.75). An introduction to rocks and minerals with fifty pages of photographs to help in identification. Also, **The Land We Live On.**

Rocks, Rivers and the Changing Earth, by Herman and Nina Schneider (William R. Scott, $3.50). A well-illustrated first geology book.

See Along the Shore, by Millicent Selsam (Harper & Row, $2.95). Interesting information about the seashore with exquisite illustrations by Leonard Weisgard.

The Story of Rocks, by Dorothy Shuttlesworth (Doubleday, $2.95). An excellent first book of geology.

Through the Magnifying Glass, by Julius Schwartz (McGraw-Hill, $2.75). A variety of experiments with a simple magnifying glass.

For better readers of 12 and up

Atoms Today and Tomorrow, by Margaret O. Hyde (McGraw-Hill, $3). A very readable explanation of the what and how of atomic energy with emphasis on its peaceful uses in medicine, agriculture and electricity.

Electronics for Young People, by Jeanne Bendick (McGraw-Hill, $3.50. Interesting material about electrons and how they work, with new information about computers, nuclear energy and automation.

Research Ideas for Young Scientists, by George Barr (McGraw-Hill, $3). A fascinating book chock full of ideas that will stimulate young readers to question, experiment, investigate on their own.

Wonders of the Human Body, by Anthony Ravielli (Viking Press, $2.50; paperback, Scholastic, 50¢). Concise explanation of the human body and how it works.

Information of Many Kinds

Big Book of Cowboys, by Sydney E. Fletcher (Grosset & Dunlap, $1). All about cowboys and rodeos, with full-color illustrations. Also **Big Book of Indians.**

The Big Book of Real Building and Wrecking Machines, written and illustrated by George J. Zaffo (Grosset & Dunlap, $1). Pictures, diagrams and explanatory text tell about many kinds of machines at work. Also **The Big Book of Real Boats and Ships** and **The Big Book of Real Trains.**

The Book of Indians, by Holling C. Holling (Platt & Munk, $2.95). Stories of Indians of forests, plains, deserts, rivers and sea. Many detailed drawings of Indian homes, crafts, weapons, warfare, etc.

Golden Nature Guides (Golden Press, $1 paperbound). A series of informational pocket guides by Herbert S. Zim and others. Each includes many illustrations and charts. Typical subjects: **Insects, Birds, Flowers, Trees, Stars.**

How the World Was Explored, edited by Lancelot Hogben

(Lothrop, Lee & Shepard, $1.75). A simple explanation with many maps, charts and diagrams.

Oars, Sails and Steam, by Edwin Tunis (World, $4.95). The history of boats, with lavish illustrations.

The Picture Story of the Middle East, by Susan R. Nevil (David McKay Co., $4.50). People, places and events that have made the Middle East one of the most fascinating regions of the world.

Trucks, Tractors and Trailers, by Ruthven Todd (G. P. Putnam's Sons, $2.75). All kinds of trucks drawn to scale and reproduced in full color with simple and accurate text explaining the use of each.

SPORTS AND HOBBIES

The First Book of Magic, by Edward Stoddard (Franklin Watts, $1.95). A how-to-do-it book for the budding magician.

Fun with Ballet, by Mae Blacker Freeman (Random House, $1.95). Photographs and simple text give step-by-step ballet lessons for beginners.

Fun with Magic, by Joseph Leeming (J. B. Lippincott, $3.50). How to make magic equipment, perform many tricks and stage professional shows.

How Baseball Began in Brooklyn, by LeGrand (Abingdon Press, $2). A tall-tale explanation that delights young readers.

How to Play Baseball, by Mary Graham Bonner (Alfred A. Knopf, $2.50). A beginner's guidebook, giving positions, rules and tips for players. Clear diagrams supplement the text.

The Little League Heroes, by Curtis Bishop (J. B. Lippincott, $2.95). A sports story that centers around the first Negro player on the team and shows how a group of boys learned to work together without prejudice.

Lou Gehrig, Boy of the Sand Lots, by Guerney Van Riper (Bobbs-Merrill, $2.25). The life of the great Yankee baseball star.

Quarterback's Aim, by Beman Lord (Henry Z. Walck, $2.75; paperback, Scholastic, 35¢). Excellent story of an elementary-school boy who is too light for the football team, but manages to save the day in the big game. Easy reading. Also, **Guards for Matt.**

Stamp Collecting, by Roger Lewis (Alfred A. Knopf, $1.75). Simple instructions for the beginning collector.

Tommy Carries the Ball, by James and Marion Renick (Charles Scribner's Sons, $2.95). A football story with how-to-do-it information and good drawings of various plays and positions.

POETRY FOR ALL AGES

Collections of Poetry

Favorite Poems Old and New, selected by Helen Ferris (Doubleday, $4.95). Contains more than seven hundred poems for all ages.

The First Book of Poetry, selected by Isabel J. Peterson (Franklin Watts, $1.95). Eighty-one best loved poems for the eight-to-twelves.

For a Child, Great Poems Old and New, edited by Wilma McFarland (Westminster Press, $3.50). Poems of nature and the seasons, of home, family and the everyday life of the modern child.

The Golden Book of Poetry, selected by Jane Werner (Golden Press, $1.99). A choice collection of favorites with many exquisite illustrations.

The Golden Treasury of Poetry, edited by Louis Untermeyer (Golden Press, $5). Poetry for all ages with delightful notes about poets and their works.

I Went to the Animal Fair, edited by William Cole (World Publishing Co., $2.75). Animal poems old and new which have lilting rhythm, with charming illustrations.

A Little Laughter, compiled by Katherine Love (Thomas Y. Crowell, $2.95). A rare and delightful collection of poems full of laughter from famous poets old and new.

The Moon Is Shining Bright As Day, selected by Ogden Nash (J. B. Lippincott, $3.75). An anthology of good-humored verse—short, gay poems which older children enjoy.

Poems to Read to the Very Young, edited by Josette Frank

Anna Elise, she jumped with surprise . . .

From A Little Laughter, *compiled by Katherine Love, illustrated by Walter H. Lorraine (Thomas Y. Crowell Co.)*

(Random House, $1). A choice collection of forty poems beautifully illustrated for children of two to seven.

Silver Pennies, collected by Blanche Jennings Thompson (Macmillan, $1.95). A tiny book of 84 short poems that are easily read and remembered.

Story Poems, edited by William Cole (World Publishing Co., $3.50). Ninety entertaining tales in verse with lively illustrations.

Sung Under the Silver Umbrella, selected by a committee of the Association for Childhood Education International (Macmillan, $3.50). This includes some two hundred poems for younger children.

This Way, Delight: A Book of Poetry for the Young, selected by Herbert Read (Pantheon Books, $3.50). A highly imaginative selection of poetry for older children.

Time for Poetry, selected by May Hill Arbuthnot (Scott, Foresman, $4.75). A grand assortment of nearly seven hundred poems for all ages.

Under the Tent of the Sky, edited by John E. Brewton (Macmillan, $3.75). Poems about animals of all kinds delightfully illustrated by Robert Lawson.

Individual Poets

Aldis, Dorothy, **All Together** (G. P. Putnam's Sons, $3). 144 poems for children of six and under.

Behn, Harry, **The Wizard in the Well** (Harcourt, Brace & World, $3). Delightful poems based on children's experiences.

Brown, Margaret Wise, **Nibble Nibble** (William R. Scott, $3.75). Choice nature poems, with delicate illustrations in shades of green.

Chute, Marchette, **Around and About** (E. P. Dutton, $3). Delightful poems for the very young.

Ciardi, John, **The Man Who Sang the Sillies** (J. B. Lippincott, $3). Twenty-four humorous poems with wonderful rhythm and use of words, both real and made-up.

de la Mare, Walter, **Rhymes and Verses** (Holt, Rinehart & Winston, $5). Poems of great variety for better readers. Also **Peacock Pie.**

Field, Rachel, **Taxis and Toadstools** (Doubleday, $2.95). Poems of the child's everyday world—chiefly city scenes—plus a few with a fairy touch.

Fisher, Aileen, **Going Barefoot** (Thomas Y. Crowell, $3.50). The poetic picture story of a boy, eager to go barefoot, who observes the tracks of all sorts of animals "going barefoot."

Frost, Robert, **You Come Too** (Holt, Rinehart & Winston, $3). Fifty-two favorite poems selected for young readers.

Kuskin, Karla, **In the Middle of the Trees** (Harper & Row, $2.75). Poetry that is humorous and imaginative, always with a lilting melody.

Milne, A. A., **When We Were Very Young** (E. P. Dutton, $2.95). A delightful collection of poems written for a little boy about his fun and fantasy. Continued in **Now We Are Six.**

Richards, Laura E., **Tirra Lirra** (Little, Brown, $3). The comical "hurdy-gurdy" tunes that have delighted countless readers.

Rossetti, Christina, **Sing Song** (Macmillan, $1.50). Short lyric poems with childlike simplicity which are a natural first step after Mother Goose.

Stevenson, Robert Louis, **A Child's Garden of Verses** (Golden Press, $1.99; paperback, Penguin, 85¢). A collection of cherished poems illustrated by Alice and Martin Provensen. There are many other fine editions.

Teasdale, Sara, **Stars To-night** (Macmillan, $3). Poems about the stars which delight all ages.

RIDDLES, RHYMES AND NONSENSE

A Book of Nonsense, by Edward Lear (Looking Glass Library, $1.95). Limericks and other poems with comical drawings by the author.

I had a little . . ., by Norma Levarie (Random House, $1.95). A gay series of guessing rhymes with each turn of the page bringing a surprise.

I Met a Man, by John Ciardi (Houghton Mifflin, $2.75). Riddles and puns in verse written in limited vocabulary for beginning readers.

Rainbow in the Morning, by Carl Withers and Alta Jablow (Abelard-Schuman, $2.95). A fascinating collection of limericks, jingles and nonsense rhymes that delight young children.

Rocket in My Pocket: Rhymes and Chants of Young Americans, by Carl Withers (Holt, Rinehart & Winston, $3.95). Over four hundred of the rhymes, chants, game songs and tongue twisters popular among children.

What Do You Say, Dear?, by Sesyle Joslin (William R. Scott, $2.75). Hilarious presentation of simple rules of etiquette. "You are walking downtown backwards and bump into a crocodile. What do you say, dear?" (Excuse me.)

Yours Till Niagara Falls, edited by Lillian Morrison (Thomas Y. Crowell, $2.95; paperback, Scholastic, 35¢). Humorous rhymes and verses in autograph albums.

Directory of Book Publishers

Abelard-Schuman Limited
6 W. 57 St.
New York 19

Abingdon Press
201 Eighth Ave. S.
Nashville 3, Tenn.

American Heritage Publishing
Co., Inc.
551 Fifth Ave.
New York 17

Atheneum Publishers
162 E. 38 St.
New York 16

Bantam Books, Inc.
271 Madison Ave.
New York 17

Benefic Press
1900 N. Narragansett
Chicago 39

The Bobbs-Merrill Co., Inc.
4300 W. 62 St.
Indianapolis 6, Ind.

Broadman Press
127 Ninth Ave.
Nashville 3, Tenn.

Childrens Press, Inc.
Jackson Blvd. & Racine Ave.
Chicago 7

Coward-McCann, Inc.
200 Madison Ave.
New York 16

Criterion Books, Inc.
6 W. 57 St.
New York 19

Thomas Y. Crowell Co.
432 Park Ave. S.
New York 16

The John Day Co., Inc.
62 W. 45 St.
New York 36

The Dial Press, Inc.
461 Park Ave. S.
New York 16

Dodd, Mead & Co.
432 Park Ave. S.
New York 16

Doubleday & Co., Inc.
Garden City
N. Y.

Dover Publications, Inc.
180 Varick St.
New York 14

Duell, Sloan & Pearce, Inc.
See Meredith Press

E. P. Dutton & Co., Inc.
201 Park Ave. S.
New York 3

Farrar, Straus & Co., Inc.
19 Union Square W.
New York 3

Fawcett Publications, Inc.
67 W. 44 St.
New York 36

Follett Publishing Co.
1010 W. Washington Blvd.
Chicago 7

Friendship Press
475 Riverside Dr.
New York 27

Funk & Wagnalls Co., Inc.
360 Lexington Ave.
New York 17

Garrard Publishing Co.
1607 N. Market St.
Champaign, Ill.

Golden Press, Inc.
850 Third Ave.
New York 22

Grosset & Dunlap, Inc.
1107 Broadway
New York 10

C. S. Hammond & Co.
Hammond Bldg.
Maplewood, N. J.

Harcourt, Brace & World, Inc.
750 Third Ave.
New York 17

Harper & Row, Publishers
49 E. 33 St.
New York 16

Hastings House, Publishers,
Inc.
151 E. 50 St.
New York 22

Holiday House
8 W. 13 St.
New York 11

Holt, Rinehart & Winston, Inc.
383 Madison Ave.
New York 17

Houghton Mifflin Co.
2 Park St.
Boston 7

Alfred A. Knopf, Inc.
501 Madison Ave.
New York 22

J. B. Lippincott Co.
E. Washington Square
Philadelphia 5

Little, Brown & Co.
34 Beacon Street
Boston 6

Looking Glass Library, Epstein
& Carroll Associates
457 Madison Ave.
New York 22

Lothrop, Lee & Shepard Co.
419 Park Ave. S.
New York 16

McGraw-Hill, Inc.
330 W. 42 St.
New York 36

David McKay Co., Inc.
119 W. 40 St.
New York 18

The Macmillan Co., a Division
    of The Crowell-Collier
    Publishing Co.
60 Fifth Ave.
New York 11

Macrae Smith Co.
    225 S. 15 St.
    Philadelphia 2

Meredith Press
    1716 Locust St.
    Des Moines 3, Iowa

Julian Messner, Inc.
    8 W. 40 St.
    New York 18

William Morrow & Co., Inc.
    425 Park Ave. S.
    New York 16

Thomas Nelson & Sons
    18 E. 41 St.
    New York 17

New American Library of
    World Literature, Inc.
    501 Madison Ave.
    New York 22

Ivan Obolensky, Inc.
    341 E. 62 St.
    New York 21

Pantheon Books, Inc.
    22 E. 51 St.
    New York 22

Parnassus Press
    33 Parnassus Rd.
    Berkeley 8, Calif.

Penguin Books, Inc.
    3300 Clipper Mill Rd.
    Baltimore 11, Md.

The Platt & Munk Co., Inc.
    200 Fifth Ave.
    New York 10

Pocket Books, Inc.
    1 W. 39 St.
    New York 18

Prentice-Hall, Inc.
    Englewood Cliffs
    N. J.

G. P. Putnam's Sons
    200 Madison Ave.
    New York 16

Rand McNally & Co.
    8255 Central Park Ave.
    Skokie, Ill.

Random House, Inc.
    457 Madison Ave.
    New York 22

Reilly & Lee Co.
    14 E. Jackson Blvd.
    Chicago 4

St Martin's Press, Inc.
    175 Fifth Ave.
    New York 10

Scholastic Book Services
    900 Sylvan Ave.
    Englewood Cliffs
    N. J.

William R. Scott, Inc.
    8 W. 13 St.
    New York 11

Scott, Foresman & Co.
433 E. Erie St.
Chicago 11

Charles Scribner's Sons
597 Fifth Ave.
New York 17

Vanguard Press
424 Madison Ave.
New York 17

The Viking Press, Inc.
625 Madison Ave.
New York 22

Henry Z. Walck, Inc.
101 Fifth Ave.
New York 3

Frederick Warne & Co., Inc.
101 Fifth Ave.
New York 10

Franklin Watts, Inc.
575 Lexington Ave.
New York 22

The Westminster Press
Witherspoon Bldg.
Philadelphia 7

Albert Whitman and Co.
560 W. Lake St.
Chicago 6

The World Publishing Co.
2231 W. 110 St.
Cleveland 2, Ohio

18.

Magazines That Children Enjoy

The American Girl (Girl Scouts of the U.S.A., 830 3rd Ave., New York 17. Monthly. $3 per year). News features, stories, articles for girls on etiquette, clothes, party ideas, recipes, nature. Gay and sophisticated looking. For girls 10-14.

Boys' Life (Boy Scouts of America, New Brunswick, N. J. Monthly. $3 per year). Stories as well as articles and pictures on hobbies, crafts, sports, nature, science, scoutcraft and outdoor life. For boys 8-18.

Calling All Girls (Parents' Magazine Publications, Inc. Bergenfield, N. J. Monthly except June and August. $5 per year). Stories and informational articles on fashions, games, personality and etiquette. For girls 10-14.

Child Life (3516 College Ave., Indianapolis 5, Ind. Monthly except July and August. $5 per year). Stories, verses, riddles, things to do, and departments on science, fine arts, music, sports and books. Large type. For children 4-12.

Children's Digest (Parents' Magazine Publications, Inc., Bergenfield, N. J. Monthly except June and August. $5 per year). Digest size. Stories and poems, puzzles, how-to-do-its, etc. For boys and girls 9-12.

Highlights for Children (2300 W. Fifth Ave., Columbus 16, Ohio. Monthly except June and August. $5.95 per year). Stories, science, biographical material, puzzles, poetry. For children 3-12.

Humpty Dumpty's Magazine (Parents' Magazine Publications, Inc., Bergenfield, N. J. Monthly except June and August. $5 per year). Digest size. Things to do, stories to read to children, stories for beginners to read, puzzles, games. For ages 3-7.

Jack and Jill (Curtis Publishing Co., Independence Square, Philadelphia 5. Monthly. $3.95 per year). Stories, poems, simple science and nature articles, puzzles, things to make. For ages 4-10.

Nature and Science (The Natural History Press, Garden City, N. Y. 18 issues per year, $2.70). Fascinating informational articles, well illustrated, plus suggested projects and a few puzzles. The magazine is sponsored by the American Museum of Natural History.

In addition, a number of weekly magazines are published for elementary school children. These are intended primarily for classroom use, but are also available for home subscription. Several have vacation editions. For information write to the publishers:

AMERICAN EDUCATION PUBLICATIONS, 1250 Fairwood Ave.
   Columbus 16, Ohio.
   My Weekly Reader, Current Events, etc.
CIVIC EDUCATION SERVICE, INC., 1733 K St., N.W.,
   Washington 6, D.C.
   Young Citizen, etc.
GEORGE A. PFLAUM, PUBLISHER, INC., 35 W. Fifth St.,
   Dayton 2, Ohio.
   Our Little Messenger, etc., for parochial schools.
SCHOLASTIC MAGAZINES, 50 W. 44 St., New York 36.
   News Pilot, News Ranger, News Trail, News Explorer, etc.
   For junior high school readers: **Co-Ed** (monthly) and **Science World** (bi-weekly).

Many children are keenly interested in the content of adult magazines such as the following:

Animal Kingdom (New York Zoological Society, 30 E. 40 St., New York 16. Bi-monthly. $3.50 a year).

Audubon (National Audubon Society, 1130 Fifth Ave., New York 28. Bi-monthly. $5 a year).

Model Airplane News (Air Age, Inc., 551 Fifth Ave., New York 17. Monthly. $3.50 a year).

National Geographic Magazine (National Geographic Society, 1146 16th St., N.W., Washington 6, D.C. Monthly. $8 a year).

Natural History (American Museum of Natural History, Central Park West at 79 St., New York 24. 10 issues. $5 a year).

Science Digest (Science Digest, 959 Eighth Ave., New York 19. Monthly. $3.50 a year).

Science News Letter (Science Service, 1719 N St., N.W., Washington 6, D.C. Weekly. $5.50 a year).

Scientific American (415 Madison Ave., New York 17. Monthly. $6 a year).

Sports Illustrated (Time and Life Bldg., Rockefeller Center, New York 20. Weekly. $6.75 a year).

Part V.

Further Reading
for Parents

~~~~~~~~~~~~~~~~~~~~~~~~~~~~~~~~~~~~~

19.

Books, Pamphlets, and a Magazine for Parents

Books about Children's Reading

Before the Child Reads, by James L. Hymes, Jr. (Harper and Row, Publishers, $2). Inspired common sense written in a warm and convincing manner.

"Bequest of Wings": A Family's Pleasures With Books, by Annis Duff (Viking Press, $3). How the Duff family introduced books and reading to their children, with anecdotes of specific situations and suggestions for books, stories, and poems. Also **"Longer Flight,"** a continuation.

Books, Children & Men, by Paul Hazard, translated by Marguerite Mitchell (The Horn Book, Inc., $3.50). The pertinent and inspiring comments of a member of the French Academy on children's book choices as opposed to those of adults.

Children and Books, by May Hill Arbuthnot (Scott, Foresman, $6.75). Intended primarily for teachers, this book tells of the reading interests of children from two to fourteen, suggests hundreds of good books for children and gives selections from some of the best of them.

Helping Your Child Improve His Reading, by Ruth M. Strang (E. P. Dutton, $4.50). A distinguished reading specialist gives helpful suggestions by which parents can supplement the school's reading program.

Individualizing Reading Practices, edited by Alice Miel (Bureau of Publications, Teachers College, Columbia University, $1.25). Although this book is written for teachers, many parents will be interested in learning how children can be taught individually.

The Proof of the Pudding: What Children Read, by Phyllis Fenner (John Day, $4.50). An experienced school librarian reports what children like to read and why, suggests how they can be encouraged to read more, and recommends hundreds of books for various types of readers.

Recipe for a Magic Childhood, by Mary Ellen Chase (Macmillan, $1.50). In this tiny book, first published as a magazine article, a beloved author recalls how her parents introduced her to the wonderful world of reading.

Your Child's Reading Today, by Josette Frank (Doubleday, $3.95). A delightful and authoritative report on children's reading interests and choices, with suggestions for parental guidance and annotated lists of books.

Pamphlets about Children's Reading

Family Reading and Storytelling, by Margaret E. Martignoni (Grolier, Inc., 575 Lexington Ave., New York 22. 24 pages. 10¢). Practical suggestions, attractively illustrated.

Helping Children Discover Books, by Doris Gates (Science Research Associates, 57 W. Grand Ave., Chicago 10. 48 pages. 60¢). Valuable information about arousing children's interest in books and guiding their reading.

Helping Children Read Better, by Paul Witty (Science Research Associates, 57 W. Grand Ave., Chicago 10. 48 pages. 60¢). How parents and teachers can help children read more easily, more quickly, and more accurately.

How Children Learn to Read, by Helen K. Mackintosh (Superintendent of Documents, U. S. Government Printing Office, Washington 25. 16 pages. 15¢). The teacher's part in helping children learn to read, with suggestions for parents.

Reading Is Fun, by Roma Gans (Bureau of Publications, Teachers College, Columbia University, New York 27. 51 pages. 60¢). In lively style, practical suggestions are given for children's home and school reading.

Your Child and Reading (National Education Association, 1201 16th St., N.W., Washington 6. 16 pages. 10¢ per copy; 35

copies, $1). Reprint of an **NEA Journal** feature by six reading specialists who explain how reading is taught today.

A Magazine about Children's Books

The Horn Book (585 Boylston St., Boston 16, Mass. Bimonthly. $5 a year). Reviews of children's books and outstanding articles by authors and illustrators of children's books, librarians, and parents.

Index

Index

H

About the Author

NANCY LARRICK began her career as a classroom teacher in the public schools of Winchester, Virginia. She is now well known throughout the United States and Canada for her books, magazine articles, and lectures about children and their education.

She is a graduate of Goucher College and holds her master's degree from Columbia University and her doctorate from New York University. For her doctoral study she interviewed the parents of hundreds of elementary school children to learn what questions they had about their children's education. Out of this research project came her *Parent's Guide to Children's Reading* and *A Teacher's Guide to Children's Books*. Her most recent book is *A Parent's Guide to Children's Education*.

Dr. Larrick is a member of the National Conference on Research in English and a former president of the International Reading Association. For four years she edited *The Reading Teacher* and is presently chairman of the Commission on Lifetime Reading. She has taught in the School of Education of New York University, Indiana University, and Butler University.

Dr. Larrick and her husband, Alexander L. Crosby, live in an old stone house near Quakertown, Pennsylvania.

THOMAS B. COSTAIN

The great and moving
epic of the Cup
of the Last Supper
...the artist who made it
...and those who
protected it

THE SILVER CHALICE

M • 7512/75¢

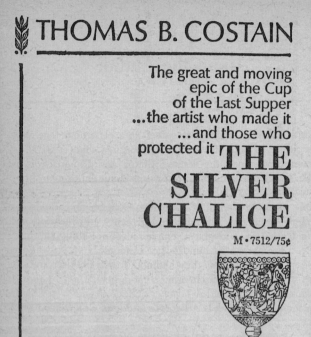

Other Books by Thomas B. Costain:

M • 7506 BELOW THE SALT/75¢

M • 7501 THE BLACK ROSE/75¢

M • 5055 CHORD OF STEEL/50¢

M • 5051 FOR MY GREAT FOLLY/50¢

M • 7502 THE MONEYMAN/75¢

M • 7505 RIDE WITH ME/75¢

If your bookseller does not have these titles you may order them by
sending retail price, plus 10¢ for mailing and handling to: MAIL SERVICE
DE........NT, Pocket Books, Inc., 1 W. 39th St., New York N. Y. 10018. Not
responsible for orders containing cash. Please send check or money order.

PUBLISHED BY
POCKET BOOKS, INC. pb

How to Build
A Low-Cost Library

You can build a personal library of the best books for as little as 50 or 75 cents a volume. Choose from thousands of the classics and best sellers in literature, biography, poetry, art, history, religion, reference and science as listed in a new guide:

Paperbound Books in Print

If you've often had trouble finding the paperbacks you want, here are over 15,000—with information on how and where to get them. Here you can locate almost all the available low-priced paper books either by checking the thousands of titles listed alphabetically by author and by title, or by looking under any of the 90 categories where selected titles are grouped under helpful subject classifications.

Order your copy of this unique buying guide today—either from your dealer or direct from Mail Service Department, Pocket Books, Inc., 1 West 39th Street, New York 18, New York.

Make checks payable to: R. R. Bowker Company. Single copies are $3.45 net postpaid or you may subscribe to the 4 quarterly issues for $10 net postpaid.